BOOTSTRAPPING

Jeffrey Cornwall

Belmont University

Prentice Hall
Upper Saddle River, NJ 07458

Library of Congress Cataloging-in-Publication Data
Cornwall, Jeffrey.
    Bootstrapping / Jeffrey Cornwall. — 1st ed.
        p. cm. — (Prentice Hall entrepreneurship series)
    Includes bibliographical references and index.
    ISBN-13: 978-0-13-604425-3
    ISBN-10: 0-13-604425-5
    1. New business enterprises.   I. Title.

    HD62.5.C6656 2009
    658 — dc22   2008047353

Acquisitions Editor: *Kim Norbuta*
Editorial Director: *Sally Yagan*
Product Development Manager: *Ashley Santora*
Editorial Project Manager: *Claudia Fernandes*
Permissions Project Manager: *Charles Morris*
Senior Managing Editor: *Judy Leale*
Production Project Manager: *Renata Butera*
Operations Specialist: *Renata Buera*
Art Director: *Jayne Conte*
Cover Designer: *Karen Quigley*
Cover Illustration/Photo: *Angelo Cavalli/*
    Digital Vision Group/Getty Images
Composition: *GGS Higher Education Resources, A Divison of Premedia Global, Inc.*
Full-Service Project Management: *Suganya Karuppasamy/GGS Higher Education*
    Resources, A Divison of Premedia Global, Inc.

Typeface: *10/12 Times Ten Roman*

Credits and acknowledgments borrowed from other sources and reproduced, with
permission, in this textbook appear on appropriate page within the text.

Pearson Education Ltd., London
Pearson Education Singapore,
    Pte. Ltd
Pearson Education, Canada, Inc.
Pearson Education–Japan
Pearson Education Australia PTY, Limited

Pearson Education North Asia, Ltd.,
    Hong Kong
Pearson Educación de Mexico, S.A. de C.V.
Pearson Education Malaysia, Pte. Ltd
Pearson Education Upper Saddle River,
    New Jersey

Prentice Hall
is an imprint of

www.pearsonhighered.com

ISBN-13: 978-0-13-604425-3
ISBN-10:   0-13-604425-5

This book is dedicated to my wife, Ann, who has supported and encouraged me throughout my years as an entrepreneur and more recently as a teacher of entrepreneurs.

BRIEF CONTENTS

CONTENTS

PREFACE

The use of bootstrapping in entrepreneurial ventures is nothing new. Entrepreneurs have been bootstrapping their ventures for generations. However, most courses in entrepreneurial finance have tended to place most of their attention on venture capital and other forms of securing external funding. Entrepreneurial financial management is not just about raising money. It is also about how entrepreneurs manage the limited resources that most have available for their ventures. Bootstrapping techniques and practices can be found in ventures of all types and sizes—from small start-up businesses to high-growth, high-potential ventures. *Bootstrapping* is the first text to offer an overview of this approach to managing entrepreneurial ventures.

The first part of this book examines the "Art of Bootstrapping." It begins by answering some basic questions about bootstrapping. What is bootstrapping? What is the philosophy that drives bootstrapping? Why do entrepreneurs bootstrap? This section concludes with the four basic rules that guide all bootstrapping activities. The second part of this book offers a wide array of tools and techniques for bootstrapping a venture, including bootstrapping key fixed costs, bootstrapping the staffing needs of a business, applying bootstrapping principles to the various processes of a venture, and bootstrapping marketing. Finally, in the third part of this book the management of a bootstrapped venture is explored. Managing the cash flow of a venture and start-up financing in a bootstrapped business are the topics of the first chapter in this final section. The book concludes with a chapter on how entrepreneurs build and sustain a bootstrap culture as their ventures grow.

KEY FEATURES

- This book is written from an applied perspective. It offers practices, techniques, and tools throughout that equip an entrepreneur to become a more effective bootstrapper and more efficient manager of the resources available for the venture.

- The book does not just examine bootstrapping a start-up. It addresses bootstrapping for every stage of a venture's growth and development.

- Interviews from many entrepreneurs provide clear and specific examples for the tools and techniques discussed throughout the book.

- Extended examples are provided in *Start-Ups on a Shoestring* features presented in several chapters.

SUPPLEMENTS

At www.pearsonhighered.com/irc, the following supplements are available to adopting instructors for download (for detailed descriptions, please visit www.pearsonhighered.com/irc). Registration is simple and gives you immediate access to new titles and new editions. If you ever need assistance, our dedicated technical support team is ready to help with the media supplements that accompany this text. Visit http://247.pearsoned.com/ for answers to frequently asked questions and toll-free user support phone numbers.

- Instructor's Manual
- PowerPoint Slides

Companion Website A useful companion Website, www.prenhall.com/entrepreneurship, offers free access to teaching resources for all books in the Prentice Hall Entrepreneurship Series, including additional activities, links to latest research, sample entrepreneurship curriculum and syllabi, teaching tips, and Web resource links.

CourseSmart Textbooks Online is an exciting new choice for students looking to save money. As an alternative to purchasing the print textbook, students can subscribe to the same content online and save up to 50 percent off the suggested list price of the print text. With a CourseSmart etextbook, students can search the text, make notes online, print out reading assignments that incorporate lecture notes, and bookmark important passages for later review. For more information visit www.coursesmart.com.

ACKNOWLEDGMENTS

First, I would like to thank Prentice-Hall for including this book in its new collection of entrepreneurship textbooks. I would like to thank Professors Duane Ireland and Michael Morris for their leadership in this series. I also thank them for their very thoughtful and insightful reviews. Thanks to Kaitlin Adams for her work in conducting many of the interviews used throughout this book and to Joseph Ormont and Nicole Brown for their help in the final editing. Thanks to the many entrepreneurs who agreed to share their bootstrapping stories with us in these interviews. Finally, I cannot possibly thank Becky Gann enough. She not only did an incredible job in editing this book, but also provided much needed support and encouragement throughout the development of this book.

ABOUT THE AUTHOR

Dr. Jeffrey R. Cornwall is the inaugural recipient of the Jack C. Massey Chair in Entrepreneurship at Belmont University in Nashville, Tennessee. He also serves as the Director of the Center for Entrepreneurship. He has a DBA and an MBA from the University of Kentucky. Previously, he held the Sandra Schulze Chair in Entrepreneurship at the University of St. Thomas, and faculty positions at The University of Wisconsin–Oshkosh, and the University of Kentucky.

In the late 1980's, Dr. Cornwall left academics to become the Co-founder and President/CEO of Atlantic Behavioral Health Systems (ABHS), headquartered in Raleigh, NC. ABHS operated a variety of health care facilities and programs and employed over 350 people, with sales over $12 million per year. After nine years of rapid growth, he and his partners negotiated the sale of most of their corporation's business interests, and Dr. Cornwall returned to academics.

He has received national awards for his work in curriculum development and teaching. Dr. Cornwall received the 2008 National Model Undergraduate Entrepreneurship Program Award from the United States Association of Small Business and Entrepreneurship. He won the same award while teaching at the University of St. Thomas in 1999 as well as the 2002 National Outstanding Entrepreneurship Course Award. He was inducted as a Fellow of the United States Association of Small Business and Entrepreneurship in 2006.

He has published articles in *Human Relations, Journal of Management, Journal of Business Ethics, Journal of Managerial Issues, Journal of Developmental Entrepreneurship, Business Ethics Quarterly,* and *Journal of Business and Entrepreneurship.*

He has published five other books, *Organizational Entrepreneurship, Entrepreneurial Financial Management, The Entrepreneurial Educator, From the Ground Up: Entrepreneurial School Leadership,* and *Bringing Your Business to Life.*

His blog, *The Entrepreneurial Mind* (http://www.drjeffcornwall.com/), is one of the most popular small business blogs on the Web. *Forbes* named it "Best of the Web," and it is linked to by *Entrepreneur, Inc.,* and *US News and World Report.*

CHAPTER 1

INTRODUCTION TO BOOTSTRAPPING

Always remember that you can create the large business feel on a small business "college" budget and no one will ever know the difference!(Kurt Nelson and Tyler Seymour, co-founders of Just Kidding Productions).

Overview

Definition and Philosophy of Bootstrapping

Why Bootstrap?

The Ethics of Bootstrapping

Conclusion and Summary

LEARNING OBJECTIVES

✓ Understand the definition of bootstrapping and its inherent philosophies
✓ Explain the various reasons that entrepreneurs bootstrap their business ventures
✓ Evaluate the ethical issues associated with bootstrapping

OVERVIEW

Entrepreneurship is defined as the process of creating value by bringing together a unique combination of resources to exploit an opportunity. Implicit in this definition is that entrepreneurs[1] pursue opportunities without regard to resources controlled. Some of the resources that entrepreneurs need to start their ventures include equipment, facilities, inventory, knowledge and intellectual property, and people. But arguably the most critical resource for all new ventures is start-up capital—in other words, money. But, how can entrepreneurs pursue opportunities without ready access to money? After all, money is the fuel that drives economic activity.

A 2006 survey of small-business owners conducted by Wells Fargo & Company and the Gallop Organization found that the average business start-up has only about $10,000 in initial capital.[2]

One might assume that having access to such a limited amount of start-up funding might hamper a new business venture. However, this is not always the case. A 2002 survey of the *Inc. 500* list of fastest growing private companies found that "the companies that were launched with $10,000 or less achieved almost as rapid a median growth rate as those that were loaded with start-up capital."[3]

So how do entrepreneurs successfully get businesses off the ground with such limited cash resources available for their new ventures? They succeed by using a variety of tools and techniques used to maximize the impact of the limited cash available to entrepreneurship ventures that are known collectively as *bootstrapping*. This chapter provides a basic understanding of bootstrapping in entrepreneurial ventures, examines the various reasons entrepreneurs bootstrap their ventures, and considers the ethical implications for entrepreneurs to consider when using bootstrapping tools and techniques.

DEFINITION AND PHILOSOPHY OF BOOTSTRAPPING

The term *bootstrapping* comes from an axiom dating back to the early 1900s. The phrase *to pull oneself up by the bootstraps* referred to American's penchant for self-reliance.[4] America at that time had a fascination with Horatio Alger's stories of self-made people who were able to pull themselves out of poverty and achieve great economic success. Such "rags to riches" stories captured what was for many the American dream—the freedom to pursue wealth without any limitations from one's heritage. Consistent with the origin of this phrase, entrepreneurs who are able to start and grow successful businesses with limited start-up capital have become known as *bootstrappers*.

We define *entrepreneurial bootstrapping* as the process of finding creative ways to exploit opportunities to launch and grow businesses with the limited resources available to most start-up ventures. This process includes a variety of strategies and techniques that cover all of the functions of running a business from marketing, to staffing, to inventory and production management, to cash flow management, to the administrative processes needed to keep a business operating. It is important to clarify three important points about bootstrapping. First, bootstrapping is not just finding the cheapest way to do something. Bootstrapping is always about creating the desired impact within the constraints of limited resources. Second, bootstrapping is not just for small businesses. As will be seen throughout this book, bootstrapping techniques can also be found in many high growth, high potential ventures. Third, the entrepreneur is not facing a choice between bootstrapping versus securing funding through debt and/or equity. As will be seen in many examples throughout this book, even businesses that make extensive use of debt and equity financing can benefit from the use of the bootstrapping techniques described in the remaining chapters.

For example, when Debbie Gordon started her business Snappy Auctions she used a variety of bootstrapping techniques to launch and grow her business.

> I had an idea. I didn't have any plan formally to do this. My first idea
> was to make a store for people to bring in their stuff to sell on eBay.
> I had a vision for what I wanted it to look like. I didn't write anything
> down. I didn't think. I just did it. I had saved up $10,000 and I put that
> into the rent, the bill and the signs and everything. We never had to
> raise any money. It is still a pretty tight business, but it all just seems
> to work out.

Snappy Auctions sold franchise retail operations that allowed people to drop-off things that they wanted to sell on eBay. The target customer was people who did not want to sell things on eBay themselves. As will be seen in more detail in later chapters, Debbie Gordon used a variety of bootstrapping techniques such as doing most of the development work to write her own franchise documents to save on legal fees; hiring college students as interns to create a less expensive, flexible workforce; and using free publicity for much of the marketing to attract potential franchisees. Debbie Gordon chose to bootstrap her high growth business to reduce her need for any debt financing and limit the need for equity financing to the $10,000 she invested into the business to fund the launch. It is important to note that bootstrap did not inhibit the growth of her venture. She was able to expand to 56 franchises in 24 states in just over a year and a half of operations.[5]

Winborg and Landstrom (2001) categorize bootstrapping into either internally oriented or externally oriented activities.[6] Many of the internal activities include those activities that allow entrepreneurs to get the maximum outcome possible out of the limited resources that they can invest in their business. Part II of this book explores a wide array of these bootstrapping techniques. Winborg and Landstrom also include delaying payments to suppliers and other stakeholders as an internal method of bootstrapping. However, as will be discussed later in this chapter, there are significant ethical implications to such a method of bootstrapping a business. External methods of bootstrapping often focus on securing external sources of resources that the entrepreneur can share or jointly utilize with other businesses. For example, these can include sharing space and equipment or various forms of outsourcing. These methods are also examined in detail in Part II. Another external method of bootstrapping is to find ways to speed up the cash flow from customers. This includes various methods for managing accounts receivable, which will be discussed in Chapter 8.

The fundamental philosophy of bootstrapping follows the old adage, "Cash is King!" Cash flow is the life blood of any business. According to Professor

Amar Bhide of Columbia Business School, bootstrapping entrepreneurs should focus on cash flow above any other measure of financial performance, including profitability, market share, and sales growth.[7] All of the bootstrapping techniques that will be explored in this book have as their fundamental purpose to protect the most precious and scare resource in an entrepreneurial venture—cash.

In summary, bootstrapping activities include:

- finding ways to achieve desired business goals and objectives when start-up capital is limited
- minimizing the need for outside financing (debt and equity)
- maximizing the impact of funding invested by the entrepreneur
- methods for optimizing cash flow

WHY BOOTSTRAP?

So why do so many entrepreneurs bootstrap their businesses? The answer to this question is not as simple as it might first appear. Some reasons for bootstrapping a business are born out of necessity. Resource limitations are a genuine constraint of many start-up businesses. But in other instances, the entrepreneur makes a conscious choice to be a bootstrapper outside of resource limitations. Whether it be to improve the performance of their business or be it born out of the values of the entrepreneur, sometimes bootstrapping is a conscious management style.

Specifically, bootstrapping is a chosen approach for any of the following nine reasons:

1. No available funding for the venture from bankers or investors
2. Limited sources of external funding for start-ups
3. A desire on the entrepreneur's part to delay external funding for the venture
4. A desire to keep 100 percent of the ownership in the entrepreneur's own hands
5. As a means of minimizing exposure to risk
6. Creating a more effective business
7. The need to look "big" to compete for customers
8. To increase income and wealth from the venture for the entrepreneur
9. The values of prudence and stewardship

The following sections will examine each of these reasons for bootstrapping an entrepreneurial venture in more detail.

No AVAILABLE FUNDING

A common misconception is that most entrepreneurs already are wealthy or have access to the wealth of their families to support their new ventures. A 2007 study released by the United States Small Business Administration suggests that this is not the case.[8] The study found very little evidence that having existing wealth led to higher rates of starting new ventures. This same study also found that people whose parents were entrepreneurs were no more likely to start a business than those whose parents were not entrepreneurs. The old adage that it takes money to make money does not necessarily hold up based on these findings.

Many entrepreneurs bootstrap out of necessity. Young entrepreneurs have not had a long enough working career to build cash reserves that might be used to fund a business. They also do not have an adequate credit history or significant personal assets such as equity in a home that would make personal debt financing possible. If the young entrepreneur is recently out of college, or in some cases still in college, the cost of higher education and the burden of student loans can limit their ability to personally fund a new business. The founders of Just Kidding Productions quoted at the beginning of this chapter bootstrapped their venture while still in college. Even when they graduated and began working full-time in their venture they continued to bootstrap, allowing them to grow a successful music video production company without taking on significant debt for the business.

Bootstrapping is also a common path to business ownership for economically disadvantaged people who are seeking to use free enterprise as a means to economic independence. Like the young entrepreneur, they have little accumulated wealth and often have a poor credit record. Whatever their circumstances, there are a great number of aspiring entrepreneurs who just do not have the personal wealth or access to credit to contribute large sums of money to their new ventures who must rely on bootstrapping to follow their dreams of owning a business.

LIMITED EXTERNAL SOURCES OF FUNDING FOR START-UPS

Various studies on start-up funding report that 70–85 percent of all start-up capital comes from the entrepreneur, family members, and close friends. The reality is that traditional sources of external money—loans from banks and investments by equity investors—are just not an option for most start-up ventures. Loans from banks are debt financing, which is money put into a business with the expectation to be repaid with interest under specific terms. Equity investors are those who purchase an ownership stake in a business, joining the founding entrepreneurs as owners of the venture. Venture capitalists actually fund very few businesses with their equity investments. One recent study found that only 38 out 100,000 new businesses reported receiving venture capital funding.[9] Another way of looking at that is that 99.962 percent of all new businesses had funding from sources other than venture capital. Equity investors such as venture capitalists and angel investors place their money in high growth, high potential ventures that can result in very large returns to these investors over a relatively short period of time. Most entrepreneurial ventures, particularly small businesses, just do not fit the criteria that such equity investors are seeking.

Banks also generally do not loan to start-up businesses. As one commercial banker stated in an Entrepreneurship class, "Bankers do not lend money to start-up ventures. Period." To understand why, it is important to understand how bankers make lending decisions. Much of the money they keep on deposit is in demand deposits, such as checking accounts, which need to be available when people need or want their funds. When you write a check to pay your rent, you want to know that the money is in the bank available for your landlord to put into his or her account in his or her bank. Therefore bankers tend to be conservative when lending out money. They need to know that loans will be paid back, because the money for those loans comes from their customers who trust that their bankers will keep it safe and secure. Bankers tend to loan only to established businesses that have a proven ability to repay the loan due to strong and consistent cash flow. They also like to see that the owners can pay the loan back personally if the business fails. They will ask for personal guarantees from the owners on any business loans. This means that even if the business fails, the entrepreneurs who owned that business will be held personally liable to pay back any and all business loans from the bank. Banks also like to see that a business has collateral that can be used to back the loans. This can take the form of equipment, buildings and land, inventory, and accounts receivable. New businesses generally do not have cash flow and have very few assets to serve as collateral, which is another common reason that bootstrapping is used. Some loan programs from the Small Business Administration can speed the process of businesses being eligible for bank financing, but these programs generally require the entrepreneur is able to invest a significant percentage of the financing from their own sources of funding.

A DESIRE TO DELAY EXTERNAL FUNDING

Even though some new ventures may fit the criteria for equity investment, the entrepreneur may choose to minimize the use of outside funding or even delay its use at all for as long as possible.[10] This sometimes referred to as *extending the runway* for a start-up business.[11] There are four advantages to such a strategy. First, the entrepreneur can build greater value in the business before bringing in outside investment. This will reduce the amount of the ownership percentage (also called *dilution*) that the entrepreneur will have to offer to outside investors for the capital they invest into the venture. A start-up business has very little intrinsic value in the early going. Businesses require sales, and even more importantly profits, to have value. Since a start-up venture often has few if any sales and no profits, it is hard for the entrepreneur to negotiate effectively with investors. If they have not been able to put in significant equity of their own, the entrepreneurs may face demands from investors to give up a significant percentage of ownership to secure an investment of funds. By using bootstrapping to delay the need for funding, the entrepreneur is better able to establish that their business has value through growing sales and even the beginning of profitability.

Second, many entrepreneurs prefer to keep more control over the business in its early stages so that they can ensure that the business remains true to their intended vision. Pressures placed on the entrepreneur from investors can sometimes take the business in directions the entrepreneur had not intended and which he or she may not believe is most desirable. Many investors are eager to see high growth that can lead to a quick exit to liquidate their investments. Sometimes this pressure for rapid growth leads to decisions to expand into new markets or ramp up production more rapidly than the infrastructure of the business can handle.

Third, entrepreneurs may have concerns about sharing intellectual property associated with their businesses with too many people. This can risk the competitive advantage that the business has through its intellectual property or even that unscrupulous individuals may steal their secrets and beat them to market. Raising money through investors often requires presentations to several investor groups before an interested angel or venture capital firm is identified. By delaying the need for financing through bootstrapping, the entrepreneur is able to better protect and keep secret critical competitive aspects of his or her product or services.

Finally, raising money takes a great deal of time and effort—time and effort that the entrepreneur may rather be putting into the start-up venture itself. Using bootstrapping to "extend the runway" allows the entrepreneur to spend time on the business rather than on funding the business. As Dr. Jim Stefansic, co-founder of Pathfinder Therapeutics, Inc., said, "It often seems that during our start-up I have spent more time developing my pitch and making presentations to investors than I have getting our product ready for market."

A Desire to Keep 100 Percent of Ownership

Many entrepreneurs do not want the added complexity of having to manage the expectations of outside investors and the demands placed on a business by banks. In this case it is not that the entrepreneur cannot raise outside funding nor that they want to postpone such funding. There are many cases of businesses that could have fairly easily raised external funding, but the entrepreneurs made a conscious decision to use bootstrapping techniques to avoid any need for such funding. These entrepreneurs just do not want outsiders—be they investors or bankers—significantly involved in their ventures.

One concern with external equity funding is that it creates dilution of the entrepreneur's ownership in the business. Equity financing reduces the ownership percentage of the founding entrepreneurs, thus reducing their share of any profits and any wealth created through the venture. The business must get that much larger for them to reach the financial goals that they had originally established for their business. Another concern with adding outside investors to ownership is the risk of taking equity funding from investors who turn out to be less than scrupulous individuals—commonly known as *sharks*. Sensing the entrepreneur's vulnerability, these investors will demand much more of an ownership stake than the deal actually requires, based on their investment. They can also intend from the very beginning to force the founding entrepreneur out of the business once they have taken financial control. Finally, a reason that many entrepreneurs try to avoid adding equity investors is the interpersonal dynamics that adding new partners or new shareholders brings.[12] Although not all investors take on a formal role in the venture, such as taking a seat on the board of directors, all owners have legal rights to vote on certain key issues--for example, the sale of the business. Even if the original ownership structure had more than one owner, adding on more can create interesting dynamics. Many entrepreneurs report that partnership relationships can be even more complex than a marriage. The commitment with equity investors is long-term and in reality, indefinite. For example, a group of three entrepreneurs had been in business together for several years. Although their relationship had been at times quite volatile, they had matured into a strong working partnership. The opportunity for significant growth had led them to bring in an angel investor. "The balance that the three of us had developed in our working relationship was instantly torn apart," reported one of the entrepreneurs. "Although the investor was a great guy, it created a whole new set of relationships among the four of us to be worked out, even though he was not very active in day-to-day operations. It took us several more years to reestablish the trust and positive relationships that the three of us had developed before our new partner came in."

Minimizing Exposure to Risk

Over the long term, one of the outcomes of effective bootstrapping is that it preserves cash in the business and allows the business to build a large cash reserve. Having significant reserves of cash can cushion the impact of sudden disruption of cash flow from operations. Such disruptions can occur due to the loss of a key customer or the postponement of the payment of a large accounts receivable. This was evident in the aftermath of 9/11 when the U.S. economy took a sudden and drastic downturn. Orders were suddenly canceled and a rash of business closings followed. Many small businesses failed in the months that followed the attack as they were unable to support the cash flow disruptions that occurred as the economy ground almost to a standstill. Many of those that did survive did so because they had strong cash reserves built up as a cushion for unexpected crises. Bootstrapping can help an entrepreneur build up cash reserves through the cash flow created by careful resource management.

A common rule of thumb followed by many small-business owners is to retain profits to build up cash reserves that can cover all essential expenses for at least 30 days of operations. Some business owners prefer to be even more conservative and build cash reserves that can cover from ninety days to six months. One entrepreneur called his cash reserves his "insurance policy" to protect his business from risk.

Although some level of debt is inevitable in almost every business, there are also some concerns that lead entrepreneurs to use bootstrapping as a means to minimize debt financing. First, debt financing can make a business much more susceptible to downturns in the economy. If a downturn occurs and profits decline, large payments on loans can become difficult or impossible to meet. A similar business with less debt will have more excess cash flow, without the large debt payments, to cushion the blow of declining revenues and profits. Second, when a business is sold, the entrepreneur is required to pay off all debts before any money can be distributed to the owners. Since taxes owed on the proceeds of the sale are typically calculated without consideration of any debt that must be paid off, entrepreneurs who have relied heavily on debt have been known to have little or no money left after the sale of their businesses. Third, bankers impose many restrictions on a company as part of the terms of a loan. These restrictions may limit the entrepreneur's freedom to make some decisions on major issues affecting the business, such as expansion, payment of dividends to shareholders, or compensation of management. Finally, most debt issued to entrepreneurial ventures requires personal guarantees by the entrepreneurs. These guarantees mean that if the business defaults on its debt, the entrepreneurs will be personally liable for those loans. The bank has the right to come after personal assets to pay off the loan. Avoiding personal guarantees of business loans has proven to be a compelling reason for many entrepreneurs to use bootstrapping to avoid the need for bank financing.

CREATE A MORE EFFECTIVE BUSINESS

Successful entrepreneur Charles Hagood, co-founder of The Access Group and Healthcare Performance Partners, operates his businesses with the philosophy that "sometimes less is more." He and his partners have always operated their businesses using bootstrapping techniques, even long after the start-up period of limited cash flow is over. He believes that bootstrapping keeps his operations efficient, thus helping him to offer lower rates to his customers while boosting his profitability. Having fewer resources can force a business to be more flexible and more resourceful. Hagood uses the example of Southwest Airlines, whose business model grew out of the limited number of planes that they had to work with during their start-up. They had to be efficient with their gate turn around to keep the few planes they owned in the air as much as possible. They realized that one of the major culprits of inefficiency was planes sitting idle at the gate. This led to their innovation of open seating in their flights, which allowed them to move planes in and out of the terminal much more quickly.

Many entrepreneurs believe that too much money early in a business creates mischief, waste, and unnecessary expenses. The temptation is to live beyond your means. Start-ups spend money on overhead with their start-up funding, including large administrative staff and expensive corporate offices. Once these businesses are operational, they soon discover that they cannot support this overhead with the day-to-day cash flow that their businesses generate. One example of this was a motorcycle manufacturing start-up in Minnesota. The entrepreneurs raised about $25 million, which they used to hire administrative staff, and build a state-of-the-art manufacturing facility and office building. However, when it came time to produce motorcycles they had burned through all of their initial funding and only had enough cash for an initial run of eight motorcycles. The impact of overhead on breakeven will be discussed in more detail in Chapter 2.

THE NEED TO "LOOK BIG"

Start-up ventures will often find themselves competing with larger more established firms for customers. This requires that they appear as capable of delivering the product or service as the much larger competitor. Jeffrey Moses, small business author, describes the challenge this way: "The fact is a small company needs to appear just as professional as a larger company, even if run out of a home office with no employees and operating on a shoestring budget."[13] Often marketing materials can be a key aspect of "looking big" as seen in the story of Charles Hagood and the manufacturing consulting firm he co-founded. ". . .[T]hey realized that they would need to create quality marketing materials to help them to *appear* to be a bigger firm than they really were. Charles went to work developing their first brochure. To make certain that it had the quality appearance they needed, they hired a graphic artist to complete their first marketing piece. The brochure was expensive to develop and produce, as it was in full color and included photographs."[14] But, they needed to have this level of quality in their materials to compete for contracts with large firms in their industry. So they bootstrapped all of their other expenses, running their business out of the basement of his partner's home and staying in low-cost hotels to keep other costs as low as possible. Only by bootstrapping their operations were they able to have the money they needed to produce marketing materials that made their fledgling business get noticed by potential customers. A wide array of bootstrapping techniques is discussed in Part II of this book that can provide the entrepreneur with the means to achieve many of the same outcomes as their larger competitors at a fraction of the cost.

INCREASE INCOME AND WEALTH

Strong cash flow that can be the result of effective bootstrapping not only builds cash reserves as discussed earlier, but also increases the income and wealth that entrepreneurs can realize from their businesses. Generally business owners get paid only after all of the expenses have been covered. Therefore, the ability for an entrepreneur to receive income from the business is a function of its cash flow. Since bootstrapping can improve cash flow from the business, it is a means of ensuring personal income for the entrepreneur and determines the amount of cash the entrepreneur can take out as personal income from the business.

Much of the wealth that an entrepreneur is able to realize from a business is based on its valuation at the time the business is sold. The value of a business is based on the expected cash flow that the buyer believes the business can generate in the future. The most common valuation method for privately owned businesses is based on a multiple of the free cash flow the business generates. The multiple is based on several factors, including historic growth of the venture, strength of the industry, strategic advantages of the company, and specific industry valuation standards. The greater the degree to which the entrepreneur is able to improve cash flow through bootstrapping techniques the higher the value that can be created for the business. Bootstrapping is therefore not only good for the health of the business, but also personally good for the entrepreneur in terms of income and wealth.

STEWARDSHIP AND PRUDENCE

The management of resources made available for a business is viewed by many entrepreneurs as a moral issue.[15] Employees trust the entrepreneur with their labor and talents, bankers and investors trust the entrepreneur with money, customers trust the entrepreneur with their business, and suppliers trust the entrepreneur with their trade credit. All of these groups of people are known as stakeholders of the business. They all have a stake in the outcome of the business. For some entrepreneurs, trust from these stakeholders creates a moral imperative to be good stewards of the resources made available for the venture. They have an ethical obligation to do everything possible to make certain that employees get paid for their work, that loans from bankers get repaid, that investors see a return on their investments, that customers get a quality product or service for their money, and that suppliers get paid promptly. Prudent decisions are required to make sure that the resources provided by all of these stakeholders are carefully managed. The bootstrapping techniques described throughout this book can help the entrepreneur to be a prudent and careful steward of the resources contributed by stakeholders. To the best of their ability, entrepreneurs who integrate the value of stewardship through bootstrapping seek to be wise and effective managers.

One entrepreneur described the sense of responsibility he felt to his investors this way, "Most of my investors wrote personal checks to me when we started the business. It really hit home with me that these people had complete trust that I was going to take good care of their money. Seeing those personal checks reinforced in my mind that I was dealing with people's life savings. That weighed heavy on me with each decision I made throughout the life of my business. I never let myself forget the trust they have given to me and the responsibility I felt to take good care of their money."

THE ETHICS OF BOOTSTRAPPING

Although bootstrapping can be an integral part of moral and ethical business practices, there is also a dark side to bootstrapping. In fact, many people have come to have a very negative view of bootstrapping due to one single practice that is highly unethical. In a study of start-up ventures, Winborg and Landstrom (1997) identify entrepreneurs who "bootstrap" using delaying techniques. That is, these entrepreneurs delay payment of bills they owe to their vendors and other creditors as a management practice in their businesses.[16] In some instances entrepreneurs also use delaying of paychecks to employees in the same manner. This approach taken by entrepreneurs, some who are desperate—and some who are not so desperate—has resulted in generalized criticism for bootstrapping in the entrepreneurship literature. These entrepreneurs are using other peoples' resources, most often without their permission or consent, to offset their own lack of resources. Certainly many entrepreneurs find themselves in times of limited cash flow, which may require that difficult decisions be made. However, to intentionally choose to use delay of payment as a bootstrapping technique creates serious ethical and moral issues. In some cases it creates situations in which entrepreneurs are using something that is not their own, such as cash flow and other resources, without permission. In others, it creates an exchange, for example inventory for an account receivable, in which the entrepreneurs have no intention in meeting the terms of that exchange (i.e., payment within the agreed-upon time period). Such behavior can even become standard practice for some entrepreneurs in their businesses, which can create a habit of unethical and immoral actions on their part. Bootstrapping should not be practiced in such a way that it intentionally harms other businesses. If delays in payment become necessary due to circumstances outside an entrepreneur's control, creditors should be approached in an open and honest manner about payments due. If any future problems in making payments are anticipated, the creditor should be made aware so that they can consent to working with the entrepreneur, if they so choose, to help him or her get through the difficult time. This is the ethical way to work with creditors. Always be aware of the impact that decisions have on the various stakeholders. For example, the business that you are delaying payments to is probably a small business just like yours.

Tom Ehrenfeld, author of *The Start-up Garden*, offered the following advice to keeping bootstrapping efforts ethical:

> Do the right thing, always. I find it very difficult to discuss ethics in a generalized way. Starting a business can push individuals to stretch the truth for competitive advantage. This can come in any number of ways. Owners might claim to be bigger and more established to lure investors or clients. They could attract employees or customers with exaggerated tales of prospects. They might claim to have certain key elements in place before they are locked down simply to calm key players. The opportunities for fudging will only multiply as a company gains traction. Founder/owners can justify their extreme behavior by saying it's all for the company—that it's business, not personal. But of course it really is all personal, to someone.
>
> So I think the real issue is quite simple. Do the right thing always. Be honest to people. Practice the golden rule. And always do what you say you will do. I truly believe that a culture of openness and honesty foments more of the same, while one that sanctions untruths will inevitably create more lies.[17]

Conclusion and Summary

This chapter presented a definition of bootstrapping in entrepreneurial ventures based on the limited resources faced by most growing businesses. Bootstrapping may come from necessity for businesses with very limited resources. However, bootstrapping can also be a conscious strategy employed to improve the performance and financial outcomes of a business. There is a moral imperative to bootstrap for some entrepreneurs who weigh heavily the sense of stewardship they have toward the various stakeholders who contribute the resources needed to start and grow their companies. But there is also an ethical dark side to bootstrapping when it is done in ways that take advantage of suppliers and employees.

Discussion Questions

1. What is the definition of bootstrapping? How does it relate to the general definition of entrepreneurship?
2. Why do entrepreneurs bootstrap their businesses? Can you identify reasons to bootstrap that go beyond those associated with the limited financial resources available to most start-ups?
3. List and describe the nine reasons that entrepreneurs bootstrap. List possible examples for each.
4. Bootstrapping can be a strong ethical approach to managing a venture, but it can also be used in unethical ways. Explain.

Endnotes

1. Since bootstrapping is widely used by *small-business owners* and *entrepreneurs* creating and growing new ventures, both of these terms will be used throughout this book. Unless otherwise noted, it should be assumed that bootstrapping is equally applicable to either type of business owner.
2. https://www.wellsfargo.com/press/20060815_Money?year=2006.
3. Greco, Susan (2002, October). A Little Goes a Long Way, *inc.com*. Retrieved on December 6, 2007, from http://www.inc.com/magazine/20021015/24779.html.
4. Ammer, Christine (1997). *The American Heritage Dictionary of Idioms*. Boston: Houghton Mifflin, p. 516.
5. Burch, B. (2005, June 22). New Business Makes eBay a Snap: Let Local Franchise Handle the Selling Side of Internet Auctions. *Tennessean.com*. Retrieved on July 20, 2006, from http://www.tennessean.com/apps/pbcs.dll/article?AID=2005506220346.
6. Winborg, J. and Landstrom, H. (2001). Financial Bootstrapping in Small Businesses: Examining Small Business Managers' Resource Acquisition Behaviors. *Journal of Business Venturing*, 16, 235–254.
7. Bhide, A. (1992, November–December). Bootstrap Finance: The Art of Start-ups. *Harvard Business Review*, 70, 109–117.
8. Salazar, M. (2007). The Effects of Wealth and Race on Start-up Rates. *Small Business Administration Office of Advocacy*. Retrieved on December 6, 2007, from http://www.sba.gov/advo/research/rs307tot.pdf.

9. Reynolds, P. D., Camp, S. M., Bygrave, W. D., Autio, A., and Hay, M. (2003). The Global Entrepreneurship Monitor 2003 Report. Babson Park, MA and London: Babson College and London Business School.

10. Ebben, J. and Johnson, A. (2006). Bootstrapping in Small Firms: An Empirical Analysis of Change Over Time. *Journal of Business Venturing*, 21(6), 851–865.

11. Berkus, D. (2006). *Extending the Runway.* Boston: Aspatore Books.

12. The formal title of investors depends on the legal form of the business. For example, the owners of a corporation are called *shareholders*. For the purposes of this discussion the terms *partners*, *investors*, and *shareholders* will all be used to designate those who take an ownership role in a business through equity investment.

13. Moses, J. (2005). Seven Ways to Make Your Business Look More Professional. *National Federation of Independent Business*. Retrieved on December 10, 2007, from http://www.nfib.com/object/IO_20993.html.

14. Cornwall, J. "TAG." United States Association for Small Business and Entrepreneurship, *Proceedings*, 2006.

15. Cornwall, J. and Naughton, M. (2008). *Bringing Your Business to Life.* Ventura, CA: Regal Books.

16. Winborg, J. and Landstom, H. (1997). Financial Bootstrapping in Small Businesses— A Resource-based View on Small Business Finance. In P. D. Reynolds, et al, (eds.). *Frontiers of Entrepreneurship Research.* Babson, MA: Babson Center for Entrepreneurial Studies, pp. 471–485.

17. Cornwall, J. (2004). Ethics and Bootstrapping. *The Entrepreneurial Mind*. Retrieved on December 10, 2007, from http://forum.belmont.edu/cornwall/archives/000730.html.

CHAPTER 2

THE ESSENTIALS OF BOOTSTRAPPING

Bootstrapping is entrepreneurship in its purest form. It's the transformation of human capital into financial capital, sweat equity into bankable equity.[1]

Overview

Rule 1: Overhead Matters

Rule 2: Employee Expenses Are Usually the Highest Single Recurring Cost

Rule 3: Minimize Operating Costs

Rule 4: Marketing Matters, But Know Your Customers and How They Make Decisions

Conclusion and Summary

LEARNING OBJECTIVES

- ✓ Understand the forces that determine the time to breakeven
- ✓ Develop the basic rules that govern bootstrapping
- ✓ Evaluate the framework for the various tools and techniques for bootstrapping

OVERVIEW

As described in Chapter 1, through the use of bootstrapping the entrepreneur is able to creatively find ways to launch and grow a business within the limited resources available to most new ventures. There are four key rules to effectively

FIGURE 2-1 Bootstrapping and Breakeven

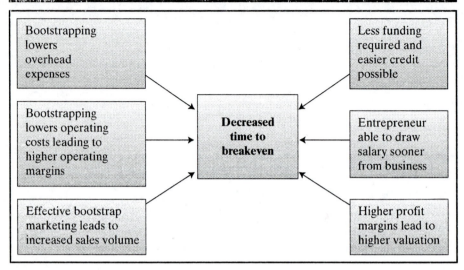

bootstrap a business. By following these rules to manage start-up and growing ventures, entrepreneurs are able to reduce the time it takes to reach the breakeven point in their businesses. Figure 2-1 displays how the two basic types of expenses, fixed overhead expenses and operating expenses, impact the time to breakeven. The figure also shows the importance of increasing sales volume, through effective marketing, on breakeven. The bootstrapping tools and techniques examined in this book help the entrepreneur manage expenses and promote sales efficiently and effectively.

The benefits of lowering the breakeven point in a business through effective bootstrapping include (1) less external funding required for the venture, (2) a shorter time until the entrepreneur can draw a salary from the business, and (3) more cash available to the entrepreneur and a business that has a higher value due to stronger cash flow.

RULE 1: OVERHEAD MATTERS

Certain expenses occur every month no matter how much revenue a business generates or how many units of product it produces and sells. Recurring costs that occur no matter what the level of sales or production are called *overhead expenses*. Overhead expenses are also known as *fixed costs*. It is important to keep in mind that these expenses do not remain fixed indefinitely. Rather, they remain fixed within a certain relevant range of activity. At some point as a business grows there may need to be an expansion of the business' capacity. This will lead to a commitment to additional overhead expenses. The first rule of bootstrapping is that these overhead expenses play a significant part in the early financial success or failure of most new businesses.

There are two broad categories of overhead expenses: general and administrative expenses and capital costs. General and administrative expenses can include support staff salaries and benefits for employees such as bookkeepers, sales staff, supervisors, and managers. The employees in this category of overhead expense do not directly contribute to making the product or providing the service of the business venture. Instead, they provide the support services necessary to keep a business operational. General and administrative overhead also includes expenses used by support staff, such as rent, utilities, telephone, software, transportation, equipment leases, and office supplies. Costs related to marketing of the products or services are also part of general and administrative expenses (Chapters 6 and 7 explore how this category of expenses can be bootstrapped). Finally, legal and accounting expenses are considered part of general and administrative overhead. These are fees paid to lawyers and accountants outside the company for services such as tax preparation, developing contracts, reviewing legal documents, and so forth.

Capital costs are overhead expenses that arise as the result of securing the facilities, machinery, and technology needed for the business to make a product or provide a service. When space and equipment are bought using loans or leased, it creates a long-term commitment that becomes part of the overhead of the business. The loan or lease payments become recurring expenses that are due each month regardless of the level of sales and production.

Overhead expenses can be either *committed* or *discretionary*. Overhead expenses are contractual and long-term in nature. Committed overhead expenses are those for which the entrepreneur has little or no choice once the commitment is in place. For example, when an entrepreneur signs a lease for office space or borrows money to build an office building these are long-term commitments that can go on for many years into the future. The obligation to pay the lease or the loan payments generally will continue to exist even if the business ceases operations. Committed overhead expenses are also those that are required to stay in operations. Even if a retail business does not have a long-term lease, for example, it has to have space in which to offer its products to the customer. In addition to costs associated with the physical space used in the operation of the business, expenses such as taxes and insurance are also considered committed overhead expenses.

Discretionary overhead expenses are those for which the commitment to pay is less than a year. Also, they are overhead expenses that can be cut back without too much impact on the operations of the business. The entrepreneur has some degree of discretion on whether to continue paying the expense or not. For example, assume that a small business decides to take out a short-term contract for a billboard advertisement for six months. This fixed cost is both less than a year and, although the business may lose some possible new sales if they do not renew the contract, such a decision likely would not lead to a drastic downturn in sales or an inability to operate the business.

Generally, employee costs that fall under overhead are considered discretionary. Although the entrepreneur may need to work even longer hours to handle the extra work, these employees can generally be laid off without any legal repercussions. However, the culture of the business can play a role in whether an expense is ethically considered committed or discretionary by the entrepreneur. For example, if an entrepreneur makes a commitment to not lay off employees as a result of cyclical fluctuations in sales, that business owner may consider staff costs to be committed. Building and sustaining a bootstrap culture will be the topic of Chapter 9.

Bootstrapping overhead costs can help a business reach its breakeven point sooner. This is important for three reasons. First, a shorter time to breakeven reduces the amount of funding required by the business. And once breakeven is reached, bootstrapping can continue to improve the cash flow of the business, thus making any needed credit easier to secure. Cash flow is the primary determinate that bankers and other lenders use in making lending decisions to a small business. Second, entrepreneurs often do not get paid until the business reaches breakeven point. This is sometimes called the *sweat equity* that the entrepreneur puts into the start-up. Third, continuing to bootstrap the venture over time will assure a stronger cash flow from the business. Since the valuation of a business is primarily determined by its cash flow[2], bootstrapping can help build the value of the business and a higher valuation when the time comes to exit the business. Continuing to bootstrap over time also yields increased cash flow for the entrepreneur while he or she owns the business

A business reaches breakeven when the operating profit made from selling a product or providing a service is enough to cover its overhead expenses. Breakeven can be explained by the following formula:

$$\frac{\textbf{Total Fixed Costs}}{\textbf{Unit Price} - \textbf{Unit Cost}} = \textbf{Units to Breakeven}$$

For example, let's assume a business sells its product for $4 a unit and it costs $2 in wages and materials to make that unit. This business makes a profit of $2 per unit (unit price minus unit cost). The overhead expenses in this example total $10,000 per month. The business must sell 5,000 units to breakeven.

$$\frac{\$10,000}{(\$4 - \$2)} = \textbf{5,000 units}$$

However, if that same business can lower overhead to $5,000, it only will take sales of 2,500 units a month to breakeven.

$$\frac{\$5,000}{(\$4 - \$2)} = \textbf{2,500 units}$$

So the lower the overhead of a new venture, the more quickly it can reach breakeven and help the entrepreneur reach his or her desired outcomes from the business.

As a business grows, the entrepreneur should always think carefully before committing to any other additional fixed monthly expenses. A good rule of thumb is this: once a business reaches breakeven, the entrepreneur should not add more overhead until the business already has enough positive cash flow each month to more than cover any added overhead costs. However there is one important note of caution: entrepreneurs should always take great care to never strangle their ability to grow in their quest to bootstrap the business. Added sales will eventually require an expansion of capacity which often includes more overhead expenses. The goal is to be both efficient *and* effective. Effectiveness refers to how well the entrepreneur meets the goals and objectives set for the venture. Efficiency refers to meeting those goals and objectives with the fewest resources possible. That is, keep overhead to a minimum, but always be able to meet the needs of additional customers. In the words of one entrepreneur, "Be frugal, but with a purpose."

Chapter 3 examines various bootstrapping tools and techniques that can be used to reduce administrative overhead and capital costs.

RULE 2: EMPLOYEE EXPENSES ARE USUALLY THE HIGHEST SINGLE RECURRING COST

For many start-up ventures, employee expenses can be the highest single cost. So applying bootstrapping techniques that can help control wages and salaries can significantly help preserve scarce cash resources. While the entrepreneur often does many if not all of the tasks during the initial start-up, employees generally will need to be hired as the business begins to grow. As discussed in the previous section, some of these employee salaries and wages are a part of the overhead expenses of a business.

Still other employees are directly involved in making the product or providing the service. Their wages and salaries are part of the direct operating costs. These costs will often vary, at least in part, by the volume of sales. The more that is produced, the more hours are needed by these employees and the more people who will eventually need to be hired. Bootstrapping this type of employee expense will help optimize operating profits from the business. With the resulting higher marginal profit per unit of sales that comes from the wage portion of the operating costs, the venture has a lower breakeven point. This will be examined in more detail in the next section.

Regardless of the type of employee expense, finding ways to bootstrap these costs are critical to the financial health of many start-up ventures. To help keep control over cash flow, the entrepreneur should keep a careful eye on payroll expenses and consider some bootstrapping techniques related to human resources. For example, many start-up businesses rely on the family and friends of the entrepreneur founder early on to help defray employee costs. Other entrepreneurs choose to work long hours, in some cases consistently over eighty hours per week, rather than take on the commitment of added employee expenses.

During periods of rapid growth, entrepreneurs may try to hire people in advance of that growth, assuming that it is better to have employees already in place when new business comes in. But, this can put a significant strain on cash flow, as the entrepreneur is trying to carry more people on payroll than current sales can support. Therefore, it is essential to develop accurate staffing plans and to implement efficient staffing techniques to minimize the strain that employee expenses can place on a new venture. Chapter 4 examines various tools and techniques that can help balance the needs of a growing venture for new personnel with the realities of tight cash flow and limited financial resources.

One alternative is to engage in employee "stretching." Postpone hiring until sales growth actually happens. This requires that the entrepreneur gets all of his or her employees on board. This requires open and honest communication of what it being asked, assuring employees that although they can anticipate an additional workload in the short run, as soon as sales hit a certain level more people will be hired. Many entrepreneurs offer perks, such as additional time off or added profit sharing, as a reward for employees' willingness to "stretch." Of course this requires the entrepreneur to deliver what has been promised. If not, credibility will be lost with employees, which can jeopardize their cooperation in the future.

Hiring student interns is another way to keep employment costs under control. Interns offer good talent often at a very reasonable cost. Interns are willing to work for modest pay as they are seeking experience and often get course credit for this type of work. Many universities have internship programs and are eager to get smaller employers signed up as an option for internship placements.

Finally, there are bootstrapping techniques that can help to bring experienced management talent into the business. Since a start-up business cannot always compete with the pay of larger companies, entrepreneurs often rely on various forms of equity compensation, which can help delay some of the compensation required by these managers into the future when the business has stronger cash flow.

Chapter 4 examines these and other bootstrapping tools and techniques that can be used to reduce staffing and human resource costs to help reduce overhead expenses and operating costs.

RULE 3: MINIMIZE OPERATING COSTS

In addition to the careful management of the direct employee wages discussed in the previous section, there are other categories of operating costs that can be reduced through bootstrapping. Operating costs include expenses necessary to produce a product or provide a service. In addition to wages and salaries discussed above, operating costs raw material costs, any materials consumed during making the product or providing the service, and the cost of any facilities that go directly toward producing the product or providing the service.

Just as we saw with overhead expenses, bootstrapping operating costs can also help a business reach its breakeven point sooner. Remember that a business reaches breakeven when the operating profit made from selling a product or providing a service is enough to cover its overhead expenses. In addition to reducing the numerator of the breakeven equation, that is the fixed costs or overhead, the number of units needed to be sold to reach breakeven can also be reduced by *increasing* the denominator. Lowering the cost per unit is one way to achieve this end.

The business in our simple example presented earlier in this chapter originally had overhead of $10,000 per month and a profit per unit of $2, which resulted in 5,000 units sold as the monthly breakeven point. However, let's now assume that operating expenses can be reduced from $2 to $1 per unit resulting in an increase in profit margin per unit from $2 to $3:

$$\frac{\$10,000}{(\$4 - \$1)} = 3{,}300 \text{ units}$$

Now it only requires 3,333 units sold to reach breakeven. Again, this helps improve the financial health of the firm.

One method that can often lower operating costs is to outsource. Through outsourcing, the entrepreneur is able to contract with an outside party to provide part or all of the manufacturing processes needed to produce the product, or in the case of a service business, to outsource some or all of the tasks required to deliver the service. Outsourcing is a strategy that can work very well for start-up businesses. Rather than bear the cost of renting space and hiring a staff, these businesses utilize the excess capacity of someone else's business to make their product. For example, many upscale coffee shops outsource the roasting of coffee beans to a larger producer. They contract with a roaster, or sometimes another coffee shop with a roaster, to supply them with freshly roasted beans as they need them to meet demand. This way the coffee shop owner does not have to buy a roaster, pay the wages of an employee with those skills, and pay for the added space that the roaster would require in their store.

In the very early stages of a business, the entrepreneur is often very involved or even solely responsible for making the product or providing the service. Outsourcing can be an important tool that allows the entrepreneur to spend more time on those activities that directly provide value to the customer.[3] Outsourcing offers several other advantages to a start-up venture:

- the entrepreneur is in effect letting others carry the operating and inventory costs of the business until they are needed for a specific order
- the entrepreneur does not have to own the fixed capital required to make the product or provide the service
- the entrepreneur is able to take advantage of the economies of scale and excess capacity that the outsourcing partner has already developed
- the entrepreneur can sometimes take advantage of lower costs found in foreign countries

An example of a product-based business that outsourced production can be observed in the start-up of a business founded by one of my former graduate students. His business made specialty cakes for sale in retail stores. Rather than invest in the machines and space and hire the employees needed to make his cakes, he established a relationship with a wholesale baker who had excess capacity. The wholesale baker's costs were significantly lower per unit due to the economies of scale he had already realized in his business. That is, since the wholesale baker was already operating at a high volume, his business had already gained significantly more efficient operations than a start-up business could hope to achieve for quite some time. Outsourcing to the established wholesale baker made the cost per unit much lower than it would be if he tried to start out baking the cakes himself.

An example of a service-based business that found cost savings through outsourcing is Bizooki, a rapidly growing web-development company founded by Andy Tabar while a student at Belmont University. Andy had gotten so busy that he could no longer meet demand for his web-development services by himself. One option would be to turn away business. But, Andy wanted to continue to grow his company. He thought about hiring employees, but was concerned about the cost and risk of taking on employees and securing space for them to do their work. His solution, as can be seen in Box 2-1, was to follow the lead of many other larger service companies and outsource much of his basic Web site programming to a company based in India. By outsourcing, he was able to incur the operating cost of Web site development only when he has projects for them to work on, and he was able to get a quality of work that would have cost him significantly more if he had hired his own developers.

BOX 2-1 START-UPS ON A SHOESTRING

Outsourcing

"I had heard of outsourcing. At first I heard it was a bad thing. I hesitated about pursuing it. Working with people 8,000 miles away seemed impossible. Then I found out there were success stories and so I got a lead through a reliable business friend. So, I just e-mailed a well-regarded company in India out of the blue to see what they could do. They were very eager and told me to send them all my projects and they would get it done. I gave them one project to start and they got it done over night. I hired them for efficiency, not to pay out a cheap dollar. In fact, the experts in India are asking for more today because they are so efficient, coming to approximately $15 to $20 per hour. The firm I work with has over 100 employees, with an owner of only 28-years-old. India is becoming very entrepreneurial in itself and I have become active in international opportunities as a result. I get leverage by spreading the workload and would recommend global strategies it to any type of start-up. It allows you to grow in ways that you would otherwise not be able to. I am quadrupling my sales now. Each year I am working smarter. I am no longer in a rush to do every task myself."

(Andy Tabar, Founder of Bizooki)

Many small businesses eventually bring these activities in-house once their business grows large enough to justify the investment in equipment and staff. But by bootstrapping part of their operations during start-up, they are able to make it through the lean times until the business can support this investment.

Another common bootstrapping tool for controlling employee costs is to use independent contractors. This way the entrepreneur only uses people for specific tasks and uses them only when demand and workload warrant. Great care must be taken when using independent contractors as there are specific legal definitions as to who can be considered an independent contractor.

There are also a variety of inventory management and process control tools and techniques that can help to efficiently manage operating costs and protect the limited cash available to a start-up and early-stage venture.

Chapter 5 examines various bootstrapping tools and techniques that can be used to create more efficient processes, thus reducing operating costs.

RULE 4: MARKETING MATTERS, BUT KNOW YOUR CUSTOMERS AND HOW THEY MAKE DECISIONS

Charles Hagood, co-founder of The Access Group and Healthcare Performance Partners, always tells my students that if he had just one dollar left to spend in his company he would spend it on marketing. Even though money is tight for small businesses, getting the word out to potential customers is essential if the business is to grow and thrive. This leads to the fourth rule of bootstrapping a business: nothing is more important to a new business than attracting customers and building sales. Marketing is the business function used to attract customers. Bootstrap marketing is finding the means to effectively connect with customers within the limited budget found in most entrepreneurial ventures.

The first step in becoming a successful bootstrap marketer is to remember that the impact of the message is more important than its "volume." Unlike a big corporation that can saturate the market with expensive advertising, entrepreneurs often only have a limited set of opportunities to connect with potential customers and communicate their message. So to be successful at bootstrap marketing, the entrepreneur must know exactly where customers go for information and focus the limited resources available to reach those customers through that medium. Bootstrap marketing requires that the entrepreneur learns to think like the customer. If customers go to the Web to find information about a certain type of business, then marketing resources should be focused on the Web. If not, then don't bother paying for a Web site. Put that money toward promoting the business where customers do look for information, be it the yellow pages, catalogues, radio ads, Web sites, or wherever.

Bootstrap marketing focuses primarily on the promotional aspect of the marketing mix. Promotion is the process of determining the optimum media and message to communicate to customers about a product or service. In seeking to bootstrap the objective is to ascertain the most effective *and efficient* means of communication with customers. To achieve this end, the entrepreneur should direct the message toward the specific target market. Who is the target market? Where do they most often go to find information to make their purchase decision? These are the fundamental questions that guide promotion. Once the entrepreneur knows where the target market customers typically go to find information about the product or service, attention should be paid to the criteria these customers use to make their decisions. That should become the content of the message they receive no matter what the medium is.

Finally, too many entrepreneurs engage in "panic marketing." They only spend money on marketing when business is soft, thinking that relying on occasional marketing will save them money. However, panic marketing is less effective and typically more expensive than a patient, steady approach.[4] Marketing should be viewed as a process, not as an event. Even a bootstrapper should commit to a budget that creates consistent communication to the target market.

There are a wide variety of media that an entrepreneur can use to market a business. Bootstrap marketing focuses on finding the biggest impact within the limited resources available in an entrepreneurial venture. Typically during the start-up period, entrepreneurs will seek out low-cost methods or even no-cost methods such as word of mouth or publicity. The goal during start-up is to successfully enter the market and begin to build a customer base. Chapter 6 examines many of these methods and media and how they can be most effectively utilized to build customers and grow sales. Many of these are very basic, yet critically important media, such as business cards, brochures, basic Web sites, banners, and newsletters. Start-up businesses will also try to maximize the impact of so-called free promotional media, such as word of mouth and free publicity. Chapter 7 discusses various bootstrapping tools and techniques that can be used to efficiently and effectively promote growing ventures. While marketing budgets typically increase as a business grows, it is still important to maximize the impact of the message on existing and potential customers. This chapter also examines how bootstrappers utilize advertising, the Internet, and other new and innovative forms of promotion.

Conclusion and Summary

This chapter has provided the framework for bootstrapping start-up and growing ventures. Most entrepreneurs can benefit from bootstrapping, as they are often faced with limited resources. This chapter also examined how bootstrapping reduces the time to breakeven, which shortens the time the entrepreneur may need to wait for the first paycheck from the business, reduces the amount of funding the business requires, and increases the value of the business over the long term.

The next section of this book will explore the wide array of tools and techniques that can be used to operationalize the basic rules of bootstrapping outlined in this chapter. After those tools and techniques are examined, the final section will address how to manage a bootstrapped business, including the most typical sources of funding in Chapter 8, effective management of cash flow in the business in Chapter 9, and maintaining a bootstrap culture as a business grows in Chapter 10.

Discussion Questions

1. How is bootstrapping related to the breakeven point of a business?
2. In what ways can bootstrapping reduce the time to breakeven?
3. What are the benefits of reducing the time to breakeven?
4. What are the four basic rules of bootstrapping a business?

Endnotes

1. Gendron, G. *The Annual of Bootstrapping*, http://www.inc.com/magazine/19990801/836.html.
2. Cornwall, J., Vang, D., and Hartman, J. (2004). *Entrepreneurial Financial Management*. Englewood Cliffs, NJ: Prentice-Hall. See Chapter 13 for a full explanation of valuation of an entrepreneurial venture.
3. Desouza, K. C. (2007, September 1). *Outsourcing and Opportunity*, http://www.eventuring.org.
4. Godin, Seth. (1998). *The Bootstrapper's Bible*. Chicago: Upstart Publishing.

CHAPTER

BOOTSTRAPPING KEY FIXED COSTS: OVERHEAD AND CAPITAL PURCHASES

[Today] you can work with a team that is thousands of miles away. (Guy Kawasaki).

Overview

Administrative Overhead

Facility Costs

Furnishings, Equipment, and Other Start-Up Costs

Communications and Information Technology Costs

Transportation Costs

Business Insurance Costs

Legal, Accounting, and Other Consulting Costs

Conclusion and Summary

LEARNING OBJECTIVES

✓ Understand the general administrative expenses of a business and how bootstrapping can provide costs savings and assist the business in reaching breakeven more quickly

✓ Explain how an entrepreneur can bootstrap a business in terms of the cost of facilities, furnishings and equipment, communication, transportation, business insurance, and professional services

✓ Apply these bootstrapping principles to an actual or planned business venture

OVERVIEW

Chapter 2 highlighted the importance of reaching breakeven in a new business. Reaching breakeven is critical to the financial sustainability of a business. It is also the point at which many entrepreneurs are able to begin to draw a salary from their ventures. One of the major forces that determined breakeven in a new business venture was captured in the First Rule of Bootstrapping: overhead matters. This chapter examines the primary nonsalary expenses that go into the overhead expenses of a business—administrative overhead and capital costs—and explores the techniques that entrepreneurs use to reduce these costs through bootstrapping.

ADMINISTRATIVE OVERHEAD

There are a group of activities and tasks, called *administrative expenses*, which have to get accomplished in any business to keep the doors open. These expenses are not directly a part of making the product or providing a service. In Chapter 2 the expenses associated with these activities and tasks were defined as part of the *overhead expenses* of a business. And the first rule of bootstrapping is that these fixed expenses determine the point at which a business reaches breakeven. The other type of expenses that comprise overhead are the costs associated with the fixed capital—building, land, equipment, and machinery—needed to make products or provide services for the customer. As presented in Chapter 2, the lower the overhead expenses are, the quicker the business reaches positive cash flow and profitability.

The largest contributor to overhead costs for most companies is the salaries and benefits of administrative staff. Administrative salary and benefit expenses generally include employees whose work centers around the functions of accounting and bookkeeping, sales and marketing, human resources, and technology and information systems management. It also includes all executive salaries, which is often the entrepreneurs' own salaries and also includes any other senior level executives the company employs. Various methods to reduce employee costs, including administrative employees, will be discussed in depth in Chapter 4.

In addition to the costs of salaries and benefits for new employees, there are additional expenses, known as the *ripple effect costs*, generated by every new hire in a business. The first category of ripple effect costs comes from the expansion of employees whose jobs are directly a part of providing the service or making the product. There is a certain level of administrative staffing required to support the added workload associated with the increase in business activity that comes with increasing sales. For example, assume that a commercial Web development business adds a new team of developers to accommodate the work that has been created by the addition of several new customers. In addition to the web developers who will be directly providing labor to serve these new customers, the company may also need to hire staff to support these employees. This may include a new sales staff person to service the new accounts, a new bookkeeper to handle the increase in accounts receivable that comes with the new customers, and perhaps new clerical staff to support the new web developers. Quite often the requirement to add administrative staff as sales increase is not taken into account when forecasting growth.

The second category of ripple effect costs are the work space, furniture, phones, computers, tools and other equipment, etc. that each new employee requires to perform his or her job. It is important to develop an accurate forecast that includes all of the ripple effect costs for each new employee hired.

Administrative overhead expenses typically include items such as:

- rent or the cost of a long-term loan for owned land and buildings (includes principle and interest payments)
- utilities (electricity, water, sewer, etc.)
- equipment expenses including purchases, leases, or loan payments
- office supplies
- communication costs (telephone, cell phones, voice mail, e-mail, Internet usage)
- transportation costs (vehicle expenses including leases or reimbursements, airfare, lodging, mileage reimbursements to employees)
- business insurance costs, including liability insurance
- legal expenses
- accounting expenses (tax preparation and audits if required)
- consultants
- nonsalary marketing expenses (promotion and advertising, market research—discussed in depth in Chapters 6 and 7)

The importance of administrative staff and systems grows as a business expands. The functions represented in overhead are required by most businesses if they are to operate effectively. However, the costs associated with these functions can create a significant financial burden for a new or growing venture. An entrepreneur trying to grow a business through bootstrapping quickly learns that these are expenses that must be carefully managed. Each added overhead cost pushes the breakeven point out that much further, requiring even a higher level of sales to reach positive cash flow.

It is not uncommon to find entrepreneurs who successfully raise a large amount of external funding, only to commit to large amounts of expenses that are tied to administrative overhead and not to producing goods or providing services. For example, a new venture was started in the 1990s with millions of dollars of external funds to manufacture a new, high-end motorcycle. Before a single motorcycle was produced, the entrepreneurs had committed to a large, highly paid administrative team and built a state-of-the-art office complex, next to a state-of-the-art manufacturing facility, to house this team of administrators. The company ran out of cash before any significant sales could be generated, due in large part to the overhead expenses that had been created. The business was forced into bankruptcy. In this example, the fixed overhead costs were so high that the breakeven became impossible to attain before the business ran out of cash.

Bootstrapping overhead effectively can help lower the point of breakeven and thus reduce the amount of cash required to start a business. For many businesses, this is the difference between failure and success. The remainder of this chapter will examine common methods for reducing overhead expenses, without necessarily sacrificing the company's ability to perform the administrative functions it needs to operate.

FACILITY COSTS

Many entrepreneurs are legendary for where they started their businesses. Hewlett Packard and Apple Computer are two businesses that were literally started in the owners' garages. As in the example in Box 3-1, businesses have been started in bedrooms, basements, garages, dining rooms, kitchens and barns.

But many businesses don't just use this type of space to get started. Many entrepreneurs continue to operate successfully out of space in their homes. Home-based small businesses are actually common. A 2006 report from the Small Business Administration estimates that 53 percent of small businesses are home-based. Given that they estimate the total number of small businesses in the United States is over 25 million, means that there are over 13 million home-based businesses in the United States. If we look more narrowly at small businesses with employees, we still find that there are over 3 million home-based businesses in this category.[1]

Molly Povolny started her business, Tanks and Airplanes, throughout the apartment she shared with two roommates. Her business made custom-designed cases for notebook computers. She ran her business out of her bedroom office, had her sewing operation set up in their kitchen, and stored inventory in every nook and cranny in their living room.

All these entrepreneurs share an understanding that beyond the cost of employee salaries and benefits, facility costs are usually the single largest expenses for a new venture. They have found creative ways to meet the need for space for their businesses through bootstrapping the cost for facility space. In fact, they

Office Space

During their initial start-up of their new company The Access Group, Charles Hagood and Mike Brown decided to save as much of their precious self-funded working capital as possible. They decided to work out of Mike's basement and garage, with their PCs set up on folding tables they had purchased at Sam's Club. Charles joked that "Mike's Chihuahua became our Vice President of Security," as he announced the arrival of each UPS, mail delivery or visitor to their "corporate headquarters." Hagood added, "We were broke but were having a blast. We were never worried that we'd make it. The question was when."

"We started out when it was just built, in a pair of cubicles in Grassmere Business Park. It was a stupid looking business park complex in the middle of nowhere. In the beginning, we were doing a lot of odds and ends projects: Web designs, content, writings, you name it—anything, to pay the bills. My background was an editorial in writing and some marketing and Will's background was in web design. We took whatever project we could find, basically. We found this company where they needed web design and we needed cubicles, so we traded. We stayed there for about 9 months or so and then we moved.

"We moved into the upstairs of what had been Patrick's restaurant. It's a purple building on the corner of 18th and Division. We were there right up until Patrick's opened, and we lived through a lot of their construction, but we didn't get to enjoy the restaurant. It was 800 sq ft and it had four different types of flooring. You came in and you had like parquet and tile and carpet and some other thing.

"Then we moved to a little greenhouse across from the Parthenon. That was ultimately about 1000 sq ft. It had four little rooms and a bathroom. We had ten people when we moved in and had fifteen or so when we left. And then, we moved in the Hillsboro Village house. We had been looking for space for a long time and it took 12 months to finally find it and live there. At one point, we had 35 people in the Hillsboro Village house. It had three floors, but it was really cramped, loud and distracting. At the time, we also had a little cottage behind that house and an annex down the street. This was last year.

"This year was about getting the resources in place. The system, the people, and the space were crucial. Then, we put all three of the places together and brought them to their current place. Now, we have sub-leases on the other buildings that other people have taken.

"It could not have happened soon enough. We now have 52 people. We were basically rotating people out and asking people to stay home or go to Bongo Java Coffee Shop. A recent hire was floating around and working at wherever there was an open desk."

(Clint Smith, co-founder of Emma)

Note: Cornwall, J. "TAG." United States Association for Small Business and Entrepreneurship, Proceedings, 2006.

were able to postpone this major overhead expense item until the business could afford to pay for it through operating cash flow. But in addition to using existing space in their homes, there are other techniques that entrepreneurs employ to bootstrap their space.

THE VIRTUAL OFFICE

The quote from Guy Kawasaki at the opening of this chapter underscores the impact that the Internet has had on small businesses. For many businesses, the need for actual space has been eliminated certainly during the early start-up stage and even indefinitely for a growing number of businesses. New businesses today can create *virtual offices* through the effective use of electronic communication. The vast majority of many Internet businesses work from home. When it is necessary to meet face-to-face, publically available spaces such as coffee shops prove to be a popular way to physically connect with partners, employees, and customers. Also, copy and mail service centers offer conference rooms and temporary offices for rent on an as-needed basis.

To save on start-up costs Matt Meents and Eric Scheel, the co-founders of the Internet consulting firm, Reside, LLC, used coffee shops throughout the Twin Cities of Minneapolis and St. Paul to conduct staff meetings, sales calls, or just strategize for the firm's growth.

"When we started, I wanted to hire 10 people, lease an office, buy furniture and equipment, and grow!" said Matt. Eric's response was always "Sell something first." Coffee shops were a nice middle ground.

Matt's home office was in the dining room of a town home he rented with some college buddies. Spending 10–12 hours a day at dining room table, sitting on a dining room chair, was not very ergonomic or conducive to productive work. "My back would ache, my wrists would hurt, it just was not comfortable." He called Eric and wanted to purchase an office chair. "I needed to buy an office chair, or I was going to be a paraplegic from working so many hours on a 1970s dining room chair." Eric's response "Go sell something." That motivated Matt. "So I did. I sold a job and bought my first office chair. Still own the chair today!"

With the explosion of home-based offices used not only by entrepreneurs, but also by a growing number of corporate employees, there has been an increase in tools that help support the home office. The *Wall Street Journal* illustrates the power of these tools to build successful, growing businesses. "Last year, Dave Novak sold $1.2 million of luxury steam-shower and bath equipment, importing wares from China and reselling systems for $2,500 to $4,000 apiece under his own brands, like American Steam and Rockstar. And he did it from his 20-month-old son's bedroom in Fort Wayne, Ind. Mr. Novak, 27, runs Novak & Co. LLC from home using a MacBook Pro computer and iPhone—leveraging Internet-based tools that make the need for traditional office space increasingly obsolete for many entrepreneurs."[2]

Many businesses, such as retail and manufacturing operations, cannot easily start a business out of a bedroom, basement or garage. They need actual physical space from the beginning. There are still many ways that entrepreneurs can boot-strap the cost of space by either cutting the cost or optimizing the outlay of cash flow. These will be examined in the remainder of this section.

FREE USE OF SPACE

Finding free space is a surprisingly common occurrence for start-ups. Growing companies often secure more space than they need to allow for future expansion. They are sometimes willing to allow start-up ventures to use this space, particu-larly if these larger companies have an interest in seeing the new business succeed. For example, a large mental health clinic allowed psychologists just starting in practice to use excess space in their facilities in the hope that as these psycholo-gists became successful they would refer patients to the clinic for its specialized programs. They would allow the psychologists to incubate their practice rent free for up to one year. Another example comes from a large law firm that offered free rent to several individuals who were starting businesses that could eventually become referral sources or subcontractors for the firm.

Just as friends and family are a common source of funding for new ventures, they can also offer access to excess space to these same ventures. One of the advantages of taking free space over funding from friends and family is that there are fewer long-term strings attached. Once the new venture has gotten to the point that it can support paying for space, the relationship is over. There is no expectation of repayment as there would be with a loan and no long-term equity stake. Since rent can cost even a small start-up hundreds or even thousands of dollars a month, this type of contribution can be just as financially beneficial to the start-up to a cash infusion that passes through to a landlord for rent pay-ments. As one young entrepreneur commented, "I 'mooched' space from my uncle's business for two years. It was space he was not using, so he was happy to let us use it. He could have easily loaned me money for my business, but this option was actually worth more than he would have been willing to loan us—and there was no need to negotiate loan terms and worry about repaying him."

A growing number of universities are setting up hatcheries and incubators for student entrepreneurs. Kevin Jennings started his business out of a university student business hatchery. "I use the hatchery for its resources—telephone, e-mail, etc. It has everything I need. The hatchery is a place to go make phone calls and get on the computer. Plus, it is a designated spot where no one can bother me. I can use the printer to keep costs low because the cost of printing at places like Kinko's really add up. I can operate my whole business out of the hatchery." Although some universities charge a nominal rent to students who use them for their start-ups, many are set to offer the space rent free. Here is how one student described her experience with the student business hatchery program at Belmont University:

> Having a space on campus to go and work on my business in an environ-ment with other hard working students has been one of the most memo-rable experiences in my time here. I have gained life-long friends from

spending time with people in the hatchery. Not only are my peers stepping out on their own creating new businesses, but they are eager to help me improve my own business. It has been amazing to see how we have come together as a network of entrepreneurs to help each other succeed.

(Michelle Wilkerson, Class of 2008, Belmont University).

BARTERING FOR SPACE

While free or discounted space is sometimes tied to some implicit bargain between the landlord and entrepreneur as in some of the previous examples, in some cases the economic exchange can become explicit. Free or discounted rent is provided in exchange for services or products from the entrepreneur. For example, an art gallery in a popular tourist community offers free display space in the store to local artists. In return, the artists agree to work a certain number of hours each week in the gallery for no salary. In this exchange, the artists were able to secure space in a busy retail gallery, and the gallery was able to staff the retail store with people who were knowledgeable and enthusiastic about art without incurring additional payroll expense. The artists still received the normal share of all of their work that was sold through the gallery.

INCUBATORS

Many communities have incubators for start-up businesses that can offer significant discounts on the cost of office space. Incubators offer space and support services often in exchange for equity in the business. Colin Polidor, co-founder of Cell Journalist, describes the advantages of using incubator space:

Another way we were able to limit our expenses was to partner with a local business incubator ConduIT Corporation. In exchange for equity, they provide us with business support services (office space, phones, bookkeeping, advising, etc). This partnership instantly gave our business more credibility in the marketplace.

Source: Courtesy of Belmont University

NEGOTIATING RENT DEALS

Our definition of bootstrapping includes techniques that help preserve cash flow in the business. Unless market conditions are very tight, it is quite possible to negotiate lease terms for space that can help preserve precious cash flow for the earliest start-up period in the business. There are three alternatives that can keep rent costs down during start-up if a landlord is willing to negotiate to secure a long-term tenant. All of these require a commitment to a multiyear lease (three to ten years is most common), so it should only be entered into if the entrepreneur is reasonably certain that the space being rented will be adequate for the business for the term of the lease.

1. *Postponement of rental payment.* Landlords may be willing to delay the first rental payment for a period ranging from one to twelve months. It is important to note that the total rent paid over the life of the lease will not change. Although some landlords will call this "free rent," in fact it is just allocating the total rent over the months that follow the rent moratorium period. For example, assume that an entrepreneur wishes to open a small retail store in January, but is concerned that like many retail businesses, most of his or her revenues come in the last two months of the year during Christmas shopping season. The landlord likes the store concept and the entrepreneur seems capable of making the store successful. The normal market rent for a store space is $1,000 per month and the landlord requires a five-year (60 month) lease. The total rent paid over the life of the lease will be $1,000 × 60 months = $60,000. The landlord agrees to postpone the rent for the first ten months to help the entrepreneur bootstrap her cash flow during start-up. The landlord will spread the total rent of $60,000 over the remainder of the six-year lease (60 months − 10 months = 50 months when payments will be due). So the rent over that period of time would become $60,000/50 months, or $1,200 per month.

2. *Up-fit cost.* Rarely is a space exactly what the entrepreneurs wants and needs for the business. It may require some cosmetic changes such as paint and floor coverings, or extensive renovation such as adding or removing walls. There are two ways in which the entrepreneur can bootstrap up-fit costs related to leasing space. First, the entrepreneur may be able to bootstrap the cost of up-fit by negotiating with the landlord to allow the entrepreneur to do the work himself. For example, Tyler and Kurt of Just Kidding Productions negotiated a great deal on their lease by renting a "fixer upper" and doing the work themselves:

> Through a series of events, we were fortunate enough to be placed in a 100 year old vacant house. It needed some serious renovations, but because we could give time over money, we were able to fix up the place for cheap and actually create a great vibe throughout the office. It was that time in our business life when we truly learned what sweat equity was, and we also grew to appreciate Starbucks closing at midnight and opening at 6 A.M.

Kevin Alexandroni, founder of Sova Food Inc. Catering, learned how to perform several tasks that helped to cut the costs of his space:

> When I started to set up the kitchen, it needed plumbing work. I have never done plumbing before, so I went to Home-Depot and bought one of those 'do it yourself' books. Businesses charge $2,500 to come and do the plumbing, so I decided I would just do it myself. I taught myself how to do it and saved a lot of money. Another time, the roof needed metal work done. So, I did everything possible to get everything ready. The professional just had to come and cut the sheet of metal and then weld it. I saved more than $800.

Second, the cost of up-fit can in effect be financing over the cost of the lease to spread out payments to better match future cash flow. Using the example of the store above, assume that the retail space for the new store required $5,000 in up-fit improvements including new paint and the addition of an office in the back of the space. The landlord may be willing to pay the cost of the up-fit and spread repayment over the 50 months that the entrepreneur store owner will be paying rent. So $100 will be added to each month's rent ($5,000 up-fit costs/50 months of rent payments in the lease), making the monthly payment increase from $1,200 to $1,300 per month. Two points of clarification need to be made at this point. First, the example used here omitted any financing cost that most landlords would likely add into such arrangements to take into the account the cost of the money. They would likely add in the cost that they have to pay to finance the up-fit in their loan on the building. Second, it is not uncommon for landlords to split the cost of up-fit with the tenant. Landlords offer a fixed amount, called an up-fit allowance, and the entrepreneur pays for any additional cost associated with the up-fit they design for the space.

3. *Graduated leases.* An alternative to delayed rent payments is to negotiate a graduated lease. The rent payments in such a lease go up a predetermined amount each year of the term of the lease contract. Using our store example again, the landlord may offer the following alternative to help the entrepreneur bootstrap the cost of his or her space by reducing the rental cost in the early years of the lease:

Terms	*Total Rent Paid*
Year 1 payments—$250 per month	$500 × 12 = $6,000
Year 2 payments—$500 per month	$750 × 12 = $9,000
Year 3 payments—$1,000 per month	$1,000 × 12 = $12,000
Year 4 payments—$1,250 per month	$1,250 × 12 = $15,000
Year 5 payments—$1,500 per month	$1,500 × 12 = $18,000
TOTAL PAYMENTS OVER LEASE	$60,000

Again, the total payments over the life of this lease are the same $60,000. But the payments graduate more slowly to better time the increases to the ability of the business's operations to support the rent expense. For businesses that anticipate a longer time to reach breakeven, this type of alternative lease may help them reach breakeven sooner by cutting the cost of the lease for the first two years.

FINDING THE MOST COST-EFFECTIVE SPACE TO LEASE

A variety of factors can determine the price of leasing or renting space. All of these can be possible means of bootstrapping the cost of space. However, one caution is that care should be taken so as not to bootstrap at the expense of the performance of the business. For example, one entrepreneur was looking for space for his new restaurant. Trying to save money, he chose to rent a space that was much less expensive than several other options. Unfortunately, the location of this space significantly hurt his sales as it was a hard location to find, with poor visibility from main roads, and limited parking.

While avoiding choices that might be detrimental to business, there are three main factors that can bring down the cost of rent:

- *Location.* Factors that increase rent cost due to location are: proximity to major thoroughfares, concentration of existing businesses, average income of immediate area, "prestige" addresses, crime rates, and proximity to mass transit.

- *Vacancy rates of existing rental space.* Higher vacancy rates will often make landlords more eager to negotiate rental rates and terms of the lease.

- *"Grade" of space.* Office and retail space are priced based on the level of finish of the building's interior and exterior. Exterior finishes and landscaping can dramatically affect the cost of space. For example, a brick building with significant external ornamentation and extensive landscaping will cost more to rent that similar space located in a building with a more modest exterior. Interior space is often rated on a scale known as the *grade* of the space. "A" grade space is the most expensive, characterized by high-grade wood finishes such as mahogany, high grade carpeting, custom doors and windows, and expensive wall-coverings. "B" grade space, while still very presentable, is a bit more modest, with simpler wall and floor coverings, metal and vinyl trim work, and standardized windows and doors. "C" grade space is very simple space that uses inexpensive materials to finish the space, such as vinyl floors and simple paneling for wall coverings. It typically will have inexpensive residential windows, doors and other finishes. Clients of some businesses, for example a high-end law firm, expect a certain level of quality in the space to reflect the status of the business. But for many businesses, "B" or even "C" level space is perfectly acceptable and will not detract from how customers view the business. And if clients rarely visit the place of business, the bootstrapping entrepreneur will go with the lowest grade of space available.

A Caution: Balance the Trade-Off of Short-Term Savings with the Cost of Moving

Planning for space can be a major challenge for growing businesses. The goal of bootstrapping leased space is to avoid taking on too much space which will inflate overhead costs. On the other hand, the aggressive nature of many entrepreneurs can lead them to take on more space than they will need at the start-up to accommodate all of the growth that they anticipate into the future. For example, my partners and I wrestled with this several times in our healthcare ventures. We tried to balance the cost of the space with the growth that we believed our business would experience over the term of the lease. In our first few decisions on space we thought we had plenty of room for growth, only to find that by the time we moved in, we had almost outgrown the space. In a couple of later moves and market expansions, we overestimated the growth potential and had to eat the added overhead our higher rents created. It is a difficult balance between the desire to bootstrap and the fear of impeding the ability of the business to grow.

An issue that often gets lost in this is considering how much space to take on and the cost and hassle of moving a business. The move can be disruptive to business operations and can hurt worker productivity. Down time of the business can lead to days or in some cases weeks of no revenue generation. Customers have to be notified of the new address and possibly new phone numbers. Internet and phone connections must be planned for. Depending on the type of business and the nature of the move, the logistics can become a nightmare.

Employees need to have "ownership" over the move as much as possible. There are details of the move that only employees can plan for as they relate to their specific areas of responsibility. Involving employees in the planning and implementation of any move will help assure that the right space is chosen and that all of the details will be thought through regarding the move. This approach will go a long way to making the move smooth, quick, and minimally disruptive.

Building Facilities

The advantage to leasing space is that the front-end cost of investing in the purchase of land and construction of the building is the landlord's responsibility—and not the entrepreneur's. This helps to bootstrap the cost of the facilities needed for the business by preserving cash for the actual operations of the start-up venture. However, some entrepreneurs cannot rely on leased space because they need highly specialized buildings for their business.

Many of the same bootstrapping principles that apply to leasing space also apply to building a space, such as location and the grade and quality of construction and finishing. Another possible source of cost savings is in the planning and oversight of construction. Although to meet the requirements of most local and state building codes architects and engineers will need to be involved in the planning and design of new construction, the actual cost of these professionals can be reduced often without serious loss of quality. Architects should be carefully instructed to the function needed from the space and the budget available for construction. It is often beneficial to get referrals to architects from other business owners who have built buildings that a similar to the level of quality required. The cost of the architect can also be reduced by limiting their involvement to developing the plans for the building. Some architects generate significant additional fees for construction oversight. In a simple building this is not generally necessary. Make sure to get a firm estimate on the architects' total fees for the project before agreeing to work with them.

Many entrepreneurs choose to be their own general contractor once construction begins. This can save as much as 10 percent of the total cost of the building. It will require a significant amount of time to supervise and coordinate all of the subcontractors. But, many entrepreneurs find that they have the time since they will not be active in their business until the space is ready. Some experts caution against an entrepreneur taking on this role due to the increasing level of regulatory complexity and liability that can arise during construction. However, on simple projects this can be a viable alternative as illustrated in the *Start-Ups on a Shoestring* story that opened this section.

FURNISHINGS, EQUIPMENT, AND OTHER START-UP COSTS

Furnishings and equipment can quickly use up much of the start-up capital in a new business. As was discussed about facilities costs in the previous section, bootstrapping furnishings and equipment can help preserve cash for the start-up of the business and can help drive down the breakeven point. Careful planning of what equipment is truly needed and the timing of those needs can greatly enhance cash flow management. Also, many entrepreneurs find that foregoing brand new furnishings and equipment and securing fully functional used alternatives can significantly reduce overhead expenses. Companies going out of business offer their equipment for sale through auctions or direct sale at a steep discount. Other businesses routinely sell furnishings and equipment as they outgrow what they own or decide to upgrade to the latest models or to higher-end products. There are a variety of dealers who specialize in high quality used office furnishings and equipment. Some of these dealers sell the equipment as is, but others refurbish their merchandise and include limited warranties (Box 3-2).

Used equipment for sale can range from commercial kitchen appliances for restaurants; to office furniture such as desks, chairs, and file cabinets; to heavy equipment for manufacturing. Here are some examples of small businesses using bootstrapping techniques to purchase the equipment they needed for start-up or expansion:

- For example, in the healthcare company co-founded by the author, we needed portable office dividers to build cubicle offices to adapt our space quickly and inexpensively as we added new staff to meet the needs of our

---

BOX 3-2 START-UPS ON A SHOESTRING

Equipment

Cameron Powell, twenty-something founder of River Rock Media Group, started doing video production and photography in middle school. He got his early exposure as the camera operator for his middle school's news show and by producing a sports highlight video for his school's athletic teams. Cameron soon discovered that he could actually make money in video work when he began taping weddings. "You have to start somewhere, and if you are trying to do video or photography, then weddings are a very good way to build a reputation and get start-up money." However, since he didn't own much equipment, Cameron demonstrated his bootstrapping skills. "I remember using a home video camera—a loner from a family friend, a camera from the school, and the editing bay at my middle school to tape his first wedding." Cameron already has video projects for.

"When you are just starting out, you won't have that much money. There are restaurant equipment and supply stores that sell used equipment. We also go to websites and yard sales. Craig's List is a great website. They buy and sell used equipment. Rich neighborhoods tend to sell great things at low prices. I go to estate sales and buy cook books. Anywhere we can find something where there are discounts and find stuff that is on sale, we go to check-out the products. Sam's Club has crock pots that we have been using for our kitchens. Since they were on sale, I bought six of them. Another time, they were selling plastic wine glasses for $2.50 a set that usually sell for $20 a set. I bought all they had and just stored them in my garage and sold them at every event I had. I could make money off of them when I sold them to my customers."

(Kevin Alexandroni, Founder, Sova Food Catering)

rapid growth. New dividers proved to be very expensive. We estimated that to meet our needs we would need to spend over $50,000. That was money we could not afford to spend. We found that the state of North Carolina had a warehouse where they disposed of used furnishings and equipment no longer needed by state agencies. They had so many cubicle dividers stored there that they offered them to us for free—all we had to do is pick them up.

- Colonial Container Corporation, a small start-up corrugated box manufacturing company needed several large pieces of equipment to cut and tape boxes. By contacting large manufacturers in the area, they were able to buy used equipment that these companies had outgrown and ship it to their new business for 10 percent of the cost of what new equipment would have cost. All of the equipment was well maintained and fully functional.

Almost every type of furnishing and equipment imaginable can be found through auctions, or by finding businesses closing or moving that are willing sell furnishings at a drastic discount. With the growth of online auction businesses such as eBay, the market to buy and sell used equipment has become even more efficient.

For example, when a group of students were opening a music store in Belmont University's campus, they did not have enough funding to buy new furnishings, CD racks, and computers for their new store. They estimated that the price of new equipment could easily exceed their $25,000 in total start-up capital, leaving no money to buy inventory or to fund their start-up operating expenses. So they decided to search the Internet for used equipment to secure what they needed for the store. They found a listing for a "Music Store in a Box." A music store had shut down in Colorado and the owner was selling all the equipment in his store. This included sixteen CD racks, a computer, bar code scanner, wall racks, DVD bins, music system, security system, numerous jewel cases, and price stickers. He had sold off all of his inventory to pay off his bills and owned the equipment free and clear. They checked the seller's references and the cost of shipping and decided to enter the bidding. The starting price was $500. Several interested buyers were also bidding on the equipment, but at the end of the auction the students had the winning bid of $1,800. The total shipping costs were going to amount to about $1,500. The equipment was only nine months old and worth well over $25,000!

The digital economy comes with the potential to use up significant amount of the entrepreneur's scarce financial resources. Computers have almost become the standard equipment for new ventures. Even with falling prices, computers, copiers, printers, and other electronic equipment comes with hefty price tags. The entrepreneur needs to clearly understand what equipment is really needed and when it is needed. Instead of purchasing all the equipment that might be useful, the savvy bootstrapper prudently determines what equipment they need to buy and what they can use as needed. One information technology consultant observed that well over 50 percent of computers and other equipment sits idle at any one time in the smaller businesses in which she consults. She advises that start-up entrepreneurs share equipment such as computers among the start-up staff.

Equipment can also be rented as needed. Copy centers offer a wide variety of highly sophisticated equipment that can be used as needed by the entrepreneur on a per use or hourly basis. Rental centers offer everything from hand tools to heavy equipment for rent. Start-ups in the music industry routinely rent the recording gear they need as they need it. It is important to always monitor the cost of renting any equipment. Understand when the level of use justifies purchasing the equipment. At some point the rental costs incurred each month exceeds the cost financing the purchase of the equipment. If the level of use is expected to continue indefinitely into the future it may be time to make the investment (Box 3-3).

COMMUNICATIONS AND INFORMATION TECHNOLOGY COSTS

Technology, be it hardware or software, seems to change and improve at an ever increasing rate. So how do entrepreneurs keep up with all of this change? A 2006 survey of small-business owners conducted by the National Federation of Independent Businesses found that many do not even attempt to keep pace

---

BOX 3-3   START-UPS ON A SHOESTRING

Furnishings

"One of the best ways to bootstrap is to buy desks, chairs, and file cabinets from companies who provide furniture to large corporations. Remember that one man's trash is another man's treasure. A local office furniture store in town has a warehouse where they have a large selection of scratch and dent furniture. If you make your selections wisely, no one will ever tell the difference. We spent a total of $825 on 7 desks, 2 desk chairs, 2 couches, and 2 filing cabinets. This would have been a $4,800 value, so we saved $3,975."

(Kurt Nelson and Tyler Seymour, co-founders of Just Kidding Productions).

---

with latest technological change.[3] Most small-business owners surveyed look to specific industry standards for technology usage rather than adapting each latest advance. They tend to take a rather cautious approach to any new technology and use it for a longer period of time than larger companies before replacing it with a newer version. Only 62 percent reported having high-speed Internet connections and 39 percent had interactive Web sites. Since the cost of technology tends to drop rapidly, the approach used by most entrepreneurs in this survey suggests that they tend take a bootstrapping approach to information and communication technologies. They secure the resources they truly need, but do so in a way that brings down their cost.

With the growth of small business in the economy[4], technology vendors are targeting hardware and software applications directly to the small business market. Google Apps (http://www.google.com/a/smallbiz/), Microsoft Office Live (http://office.microsoft.com/en-us/officelive/FX101945631033.aspx), and startupnation.com (http://startupnation.com/) offer a variety of services and tools tailored for small business including communication tools, publishing tools, and Web management. Student entrepreneur Kevin Jennings, founder of soundAFX, says, "I use Google's business applications service for my e-mail. This allows my organization to use Google's email platform with a customized domain name free of charge. It looks professional to potential clients, and I am using a familiar email platform with great features. I also use the web-based calendar and spreadsheet software to share and collaborate with my partner."

An important caution is to make sure that you won't quickly outgrow the technologies you choose. Migration to another set of software tools is not always easy. It is not unusual for small businesses to find it impossible to review financial statements for weeks or even several months when upgrading accounting systems. Such an information gap can prove detrimental to navigating the growth of an entrepreneurial venture. Try to envision your needs for the next two to three years to make sure the applications chosen remain appropriate for the business as it grows and becomes more complex. For example, if a business is planning to open new locations over the next three years, the owner should choose software that easily allows for analysis of the performance of each location and provide aggregate data for the business as a whole.

To anticipate information needs more accurately, software and hardware planning are an integral part of business planning. Software and hardware should be evaluated during the planning process to ensure that it can adequately meet the needs of a growing staff and an increasingly complex business operation. Bootstrapping technology should therefore be viewed over the life and utility of that technology for a specific business, not just in terms of the immediate cash outlay. As an example, consider the decision to purchase a phone system. Smaller phone systems have an upper limit to the number of extensions they can support. It would be unwise to purchase a phone system that does not have the capacity to handle the additional employees the business plan forecasts for the next year. The cost of frequent upgrades in any technology will generally far exceed any cost savings from a smaller capacity system. Although phone systems can be quite expensive, the installation of smaller systems may not require a technician, thus helping to bootstrap the cost.

Each additional traditional phone line the company carries is a new fixed cost; therefore, someone in the business should monitor phone line usage during the day to assure that the business has enough, but not too many, phone lines. With increasing competition among phone service providers, shopping for the best rates among the various local carriers can help keep communications costs down. A 2005 survey of small-business owners conducted by the National Federation of Independent Businesses found that 40 percent of entrepreneurs surveyed regularly shop for their phone service among available carriers.[5]

Internet-based phone services, also known as Voice over Internet Protocol (VoIP) can significantly reduce the cost of phone lines, particularly for businesses that have a heavy use of long distance and international calling. One start-up Web development company found that VoIP worked well when communicating with developers he subcontracted with in India, keeping his costs reasonably low for the long and frequent teleconference calls he had to make for each new project. In its early forms, VoIP had a very poor sound quality and spotty reliability. However, recent improvements in technology have made it an attractive alternative. VoIP service providers tend to specialize and tailor features for certain types of uses, so it is important to find a vendor that fits the usage needs of the business.[6]

Cell phones have become a standard tool for small business. A 2005 survey found that almost 80 percent of small businesses have at least one business cell phone.[7] Increasingly, many entrepreneurs forgo traditional landlines and use only cell phones for their business needs. They are particularly useful for entrepreneurs who do not work in a fixed office. For example, a small painting contractor found that cell phones were the best option since he spent much of his time supervising and often working with his painting crews. When potential customers called his cell phone, he was able to schedule appointments to make bids on new projects. He had found that when using his old landline, he had to rely on voice mail. This led to many inquiries not being responded to quickly enough to satisfy customer expectations. He missed out on opportunities to bid on projects simply because competitors were able to respond to inquiries more quickly.

Although relying on cell phones can be a cost-effective approach to communication for many small businesses, there are some limitations to keep in mind:

- Traditional landlines are the best option for businesses that need a centralized point of communication.

- Currently, cell phone numbers are not listed in standard directories, making it more difficult for potential customers to find the entrepreneur's business cell number.

- This is further complicated if traditional yellow page directories are how people still search for a particular type of business. Even most online phone directories tend to draw from landline listings.

- Although coverage areas have improved, reliability of service is still a concern with cell phone use.

TRANSPORTATION COSTS

In our mobile society, transportation is a significant part of most business operations, be it traveling to meet with a customer, making deliveries, picking up supplies, flying to conferences, and of course, commuting to work. A 2004 survey found that 82 percent of entrepreneurs owned at least one vehicle for their business.[8] Older vehicles can be purchased for substantially less than new ones, so many entrepreneurs try to bootstrap their transportation costs by purchasing used vehicles. It is a myth that new cars lose much of their value as soon as they are driven off the lot,[9] but vehicles that are a few years old do cost a fraction of new or almost new ones. Leasing vehicles can help spread out the cash flow if a new vehicle is required for a specific reason.

When overnight travel is required, low cost alternatives for airfare and lodging offer opportunities to bootstrap these expenses. Charles Hagood and Mike Brown of The Access Group (highlighted earlier in this chapter) keep travel costs down by flying the discount airline Southwest and staying in hotels such as Hampton Inns for Charles and Microtel for the more conservative Mike. Although their business is now quite successful they have chosen to continue the practice of bootstrapping their travel to build a bootstrapping culture within their business. This will be discussed in Chapter 10.

BUSINESS INSURANCE COSTS

According to a 2002 survey of entrepreneurs, the most common types of business insurance expenses (outside of employee benefits, which will be discussed in Chapter 4) "are property damage, workers' compensation, and premise liability (covering slips and falls, etc.). Owners reported that the median spent on insurance including workers' and unemployment compensation is 7 percent of gross sales."[10] Since insurance premiums are generally not negotiable, there are several steps that this survey found that entrepreneurs use to keep premiums down or at least to keep them from rising too rapidly:

- *Changing insurers (34 percent of respondents).* insurance companies will often be more aggressive with lower rates to attract new clients.

- *Increasing deductibles (30 percent).* by taking on more risk with higher deductibles a business will in effect partially insure themselves for the risk of the deductible.

- *Changing agents or brokers (25 percent).* just as insurance companies seek new business with lower prices, so too do some agents by taking lower fees in the first year of coverage.

- *Changing business operations to reduce claims risk (18 percent).* new safety policies, new business practices, discontinuing certain higher-risk activities, and so forth are all ways to potentially cut premiums. Some insurance companies will work with a business to identify opportunities to reduce risk.

- *Reducing or eliminating coverage (17 percent).* this is generally not advisable, as it opens up the business to significant risk. Bootstrapping should always weigh the cost-benefits of any savings.

LEGAL, ACCOUNTING, AND OTHER CONSULTING COSTS

In any given year, the majority of small businesses (65 percent according to one recent survey[11]) will need the service of a lawyer, and most entrepreneurs use an outside CPA to prepare their tax returns. The median legal expense of those small businesses needing an attorney was between $4,000 and $5,000.[12] Accountant expenses even for routine business tax returns can easily add hundreds or even thousands of dollars to the cost of outside consultants and advisors. Therefore, finding ways to bootstrap these expenses without exposing the business to any undue risk can have a significant impact on financial performance and cash flow (Box 3-4).

HIRING ATTORNEYS AND CPAS

Establishing relationships with attorneys and CPAs that can best meet the needs of the entrepreneur and the business is the first step in managing these expenses. The following steps should be taken to help choose the optimum professional consultants and create clear expectations on how entrepreneurs want these professionals to work with them and their company[13]:

- Get referrals for accountants and lawyers from other entrepreneurs. Listen to why they are satisfied with these professionals. Choose two to three that seem to meet the needs of the company, its culture, and the personality of the entrepreneur, to interview.

BOX 3-4   START-UPS ON A SHOESTRING

Start-Up Costs

Uniform Franchise Offering Circular (UFOC) is a required document for businesses that sell franchises. A franchisor must provide one to each prospective franchisee. It is a highly structured legal document that provides information on the franchisor's background, any outstanding or past litigation, a complete list and history of all investors in the franchising company and their compensation, and so forth. It also describes in great detail the nature of the franchise venture, what is provided by the franchisor, and what is expected from the franchisee. Debbie Gordon, founder of Snappy Auctions, decided to bootstrap her new venture by developing the UFOC herself.

"People usually hire lawyers and spend $100,000–$150,000 to get them written," said Debbie. "I wrote my own. The table of contents is the same for every franchise. The sections are the same. Every franchise has to be the same. The first part is in simple terms and the back is all in legal words. It took a couple months to do." She also wrote the Operations Manual for her franchise businesses to use, which is also required.

- In the interview, evaluate personality and fit of the entrepreneur. Are they good listeners? Are they easy to talk to? Do they seem to clearly understand the needs of the entrepreneur and the business? Do they appear trustworthy? Treat the interview as if the professional was being considered for a senior management position in the business. The entrepreneur may need to work very closely with these professionals during what could be some of the most difficult challenges facing a business (for example, IRS audits, litigation, selling the business, etc.). It is critical that the entrepreneur has a sense of comfort and trust with these professionals if and when these critical issues arise.

- If the entrepreneur has partners and/or senior level managers, all should be involved in interviewing prospective attorneys and CPAs. The entire team will likely have involvement with these professionals, so the fit with the entire team should be assessed.

- It is preferable that professionals have working knowledge and experience in the industry in which the entrepreneur's business operates. There are specific laws and tax regulations for almost every industry sector. Such knowledge improves the ability of lawyers and CPAs to advise the entrepreneur. It can also help reduce the cost of their services. Since they most often bill by the hour, professionals may bill the entrepreneur for time spent researching the industry if they do not have experience in that industry.

- Part of the interviews should be a discussion of billing policies. Often, billing practices *and rates* are negotiable before a relationship is established. They may be willing to cap certain services, for example tax return preparation or preparation of standard contracts used in the course of business. Also be clear as to any cost constraints and budgets for standard accounting and legal work. If the attorney or CPA sees the growth potential in a new venture, they may even be willing to drastically cut or even waive some early fees. They will sometimes do this if they believe the venture will create sizable fees as it succeeds and grows. This is a good reason to share business plans with attorneys and CPAs.

- Finally, determine how important the new account will be to the attorney or CPA. Pay attention to how they react to your interest in interviewing them for this engagement. Note how quickly they return phone calls. Entrepreneurs should work with professional firms that value their business.

Once engagements with law and accounting firms are established, the entrepreneur can bootstrap these expenses by properly managing the interactions with these professional consultants. The following steps can help reduce the overall cost of professional services without sacrificing the fundamental quality of the work performed:

- Prepare for all meetings with attorneys and CPAs in advance. These professionals often bill by the hour, so the entrepreneur can help make any meetings more efficient and productive with careful preparation.

- It is advisable to batch issues together into a single meeting whenever possible. This will also help make meetings more efficient. It will cost more to have several meetings on minor issues compared to a single meeting where several issues can be addressed in one sitting.

- The entrepreneur's staff can perform many tasks that will cut down on the actual billable hours charged by the firm. Entrepreneurs should insist their staff be allowed to perform routine tasks, rather than paying for the law or accounting firm's staff to do this work.

- Most professionals have significant charges for what are called *non-time charges*. This can include making copies of documents, using delivery services, and so forth. One entrepreneur described it this way, "Once I realized that my attorney was charging me $2.50 for every page of a copied document and $50 to deliver document across town, I started telling him that I would make the copies and my employees could pick-up or deliver all documents. It actually saved me hundreds of dollars every year."

- Significant billable meeting time can be spent getting an attorney or CPA "up to speed" on the current state of the business. Most firms do not charge for reading e-mails, so many entrepreneurs have found that they can shorten billable time with professionals by sending them monthly or quarterly updates on their business and the issues they are facing.

- If there are concerns or confusion about bills received for services from professional consultants, discuss them with them openly. If the consultants did work that was not approved, they should reverse those charges. If they are unwilling to have open discussions, it may be time to seek out a new firm to work with.

There are Web-based services that can greatly reduce the cost of routine professional services. For example, Web sites like legalzoom.com can assist with simple incorporations, provide basic leases, and guide the process of simple intellectual property protection. More complex issues will still require engaging professional service providers. But, many attorneys who routinely work with entrepreneurs are beginning to recommend the use of Web sites like legalzoom.com for the routine needs of start-up ventures with limited budgets. They do not view Web sites as a replacement for their services, but as a means to save the entrepreneur's limited funds for more complex legal work that inevitably will arise. Accounting software packages can also be a means of reducing the total cost of using the services of a CPA. When properly used, these packages can produce reports that make tax preparation much simpler, thus helping to bootstrap the total cost.

Conclusion and Summary

This chapter has examined ways to bootstrap the various nonsalary expenses associated with the administrative functions of an entrepreneurial venture, including: the cost of facilities for business; the purchase of furnishings and equipment; communication equipment and fees, transportation costs, including vehicle expenses; business insurance expenses; and the costs associated with legal and accounting services necessary for almost any business. Bootstrapping these costs can help reduce the start-up expenses of a business and help it reach breakeven much sooner—two factors that can contribute to the success or failure of many new businesses.

Chapter 4 will shift attention to bootstrapping what is usually the largest single expenses category for any business—employee salaries and benefits. This includes employee costs associated with the administrative overhead of the business and employee expenses tied directly to making the product or providing the service.

Discussion Questions

1. What types of expenses comprise the administrative overhead of a business?
2. What are the various methods an entrepreneur can use to bootstrap the facilities costs for a venture?
3. Discuss the various means to bootstrap the cost of furnishings and equipment, communication, transportation, and business insurance.
4. There are various steps that can be taken to bootstrap professional legal and accounting services. Develop a plan for how you will hire a professional to provide these services and how you will manage them once engaged. Describe how each part of the plan will help to bootstrap.

Endnotes

1. http://www.sba.gov/advo/research/.
2. Bounds, G. (2007). Online Tools Give Home-Based Firms Office-Style Services. *The Wall Street Journal Online*. Retrieved on December 17, 2007 from http://online.wsj.com/public/article/SB118946365212923064.html?mod=blog.

3. http://www.nfib.com/object/sbPolls.

4. The Small Business Administration estimates that there are about 650,000 new small business started every year: http://www.sba.gov/advo/.

5. http://www.nfib.com/object/sbPolls.

6. See http://www.inc.com/magazine/20060601/handson-tools.html for a recent review.

7. http://www.nfib.com/object/sbPolls.

8. Ibid.

9. Lott, J. (2007). Driving the Lemon Myth off the Lot. *Foxbusiness.com*. Retrieved on December 19, 2007 from http://www.foxbusiness.com/article/driving-lemon-myth-lot-290898.html.

10. http://www.nfib.com/object/sbPolls.

11. Ibid.

12. Ibid.

13. Bagley, C. and Dauchy, C. (2007). *The Entrepreneur's Guide to Business Law*. 3rd edition. Belmont, CA: South-Western.

STAFFING AND HUMAN RESOURCE BOOTSTRAPPING

What does every big business have that a small one does not? Staff. We found out that we did not need to pay a full staff of workers every day. Instead all the workers that are on a video shoot with us are freelance (we pay them a set day rate). We do not have to worry about having a full staff on hand waiting for a shoot; we simply set the production schedule, which is then emailed with call sheets and information on the shoot.

What about normal 'office' duties that need to be taken care of? We need to have someone answer phones and get paperwork done and keep our books balanced. So how does this all work? We cannot really afford to pay anyone on salary. Instead, we find a friend around the college campus who you love to be around and pay them to come over and work for a couple hours, or give them a gift card to a restaurant for helping you out. Friends will love being a part of growing your business. (Kurt Nelson and Tyler Seymour, co-founders of Just Kidding Productions)

Overview

Types of Employee Costs

Employee Stretching

Timing of Hiring

The Virtual Team

Employee Leasing and Temporary Employees

Using Student Interns

Nonsalary Compensation
Other Compensation and Benefits
Employee Training
Payroll Costs
Conclusion and Summary

LEARNING OBJECTIVES

✓ Understand the expenses associated with having employees in a business and how bootstrapping can provide costs savings for small and growing entrepreneurial companies

✓ Explain how an entrepreneur can bootstrap a business in terms of the employee costs such as nonsalary compensation and benefits, employee training, and payroll processing expenses

✓ Apply these bootstrapping principles to an actual or planned business venture

OVERVIEW

For most entrepreneurial ventures, the single largest category of expenses is employee pay (salaries and hourly wages), the benefits offered to these employees, and the indirect costs of having employees. Employee pay includes both overhead expenses and expenses directly tied to making products or providing services. Pay included in overhead will have a direct effect on breakeven, while pay tied to direct expenses will help determine the operating profit margin for the business. Therefore, any entrepreneur trying to bootstrap a business has to find ways to influence employee pay in order to have a meaningful impact on cash flow.

In this chapter, we examine the various categories of pay and benefits and techniques that entrepreneurs employ to help bootstrap the cost of managing and employing the human resources required to operate a successful entrepreneurial venture. To understand the essential elements of bootstrapping these types of costs, we first need to understand the various types of employee costs that are associated with operating almost every business.

TYPES OF EMPLOYEE COSTS

Throughout much of this chapter various methods of bootstrapping employee costs will be examined. Employee costs are categorized as *administrative* and *direct*, and as *hourly* and *salaried*. Understanding how these costs behave and how they impact cash flow will determine which can be reduced or eliminated through bootstrapping techniques.

As discussed in the previous chapters, overhead expenses have a significant impact on the breakeven point of a business. Chapter 3 examined how nonsalary administrative overhead can be reduced through bootstrapping by reducing the amount of revenue required to break even. For most businesses, the largest part of administrative overhead expenses is comprised of salaries and benefits of administrative employees. Administrative employees are typically those who perform jobs in the functional areas of accounting and finance, human resources, information systems, and marketing. It also includes the compensation of the lead executives, which typically includes the founding entrepreneurs and any other general management personnel that are part of the leadership team. Administrative staff includes all of those employees and functions that are not directly tied to making a product or providing the service offered by the business.

The administrative functions that these employees perform are critical to the operation of any business. Those employees performing accounting and finance functions are responsible for making sure that accounts receivable are collected to ensure timely cash flow from sales, and that bills and payroll are paid on a timely basis. Those performing the marketing function seek new customers to help support the growth of the business. Human resource functions assure legal compliance for hiring and firing and that employees are recruited and trained so they can perform critical jobs needed during expansion. Because information has become a vital resource for every business, the function of designing, setting up, and monitoring information systems has also become an integral part of the administrative functions of even small businesses.

In a large business, these functions are performed by specialized staff, often within separate departments of the organization. The challenge to the entrepreneur is that there is rarely enough capital to support hiring specific employees to perform each of these functions. Because they are all part of the administrative expenses, these salaries become part of the overhead that must be covered before a business reaches profitability. Hiring too large an administrative staff during the early stages of a venture might make reaching breakeven an impossible goal. Therefore, bootstrapping these functions is essential to ensure that these vital functions are performed, but that doing so will not put the venture in an untenable financial position. A common cause of business failure is running out of cash before the venture reaches operational breakeven. Excessive overhead will only hasten what actually can be an avoidable cause of failure.

Direct employees are those whose jobs tie them directly to making the product or providing the services for a business. Carpenters in a cabinet making shop and servers in a restaurant are examples of direct employees. The wages and benefits of direct employees are included in the cost of the product or the cost of providing a service. In theory, the cost of direct employees will vary directly with the number of units of products or services that a business produces. The direct employees are only scheduled to work when there is work that will generate revenues. In our examples, the cabinet shop only schedules carpenters to work when there are orders for cabinets to be built, and the restaurant owner only keeps servers working as long as there are customers in the restaurant. In these examples, the cost of these employees varies directly with the revenues of the business.

Other entrepreneurs may choose to keep employees working regardless of short-term demand fluctuations. The cabinet worker may schedule carpenters to work forty hours a week even if there is not forty hours of work for each of them to perform in building cabinets. The restaurant owner may keep servers working regardless of how busy the restaurant actually is each day. Entrepreneurs may do this for ethical reasons—they believe that they have committed to their employees a certain number of hours each week and they intend to fulfill that commitment. The entrepreneur may also do this because labor markets are highly competitive, and if they do not keep offering consistent hours the workers may leave to work for a competitor. Regardless of the reason, the entrepreneur loses the most basic means of bootstrapping direct employee costs—that is, linking hours worked for employees to directly meet demand. However, just as with the fixed cost of administrative salaries, there are still many ways for entrepreneurs to bootstrap employee costs.

In many small businesses, employees perform multiple roles and may even hold more than one job. This is called a *mixed employee cost*. For example, assume that in a small Web development business an employee spends half of his or her time selling to prospective customers and half of his or her time developing Web sites for those customers. He or she is paid a fixed salary for the twenty hours he or she spends selling each week and is paid hourly for the time he or she spends actively developing Web sites. In this example, part of this employee's time is administrative and part is direct, meaning that his or her time should be allocated between these two categories of employee costs to accurately reflect how his or her time is being spent.

Another way of categorizing employees is by how they are paid. Generally, most employees are either paid a fixed salary or paid based on the hours that they work. Hourly workers must be paid overtime rate of one and one half times their normal hourly rate for any hours they work over forty each week. Salaried workers can be either exempt or nonexempt from the requirement to pay overtime. Employees who are exempt from overtime pay requirements include administrative staff, executives, professionals, and employees whose job is related to sales. A 2003 survey found that hourly pay is the dominant form of payment for both full-time and part-time employees in small businesses.[1] Entrepreneurs and small-business owners seem to find that hourly pay gives them the flexibility to have employees work only when needed. Carefully limiting the hours employees work to time they are contributing to creating products or services is the most common approach entrepreneurs use to bootstrap employee costs.

EMPLOYEE STRETCHING

Adding more employees usually goes hand-in-hand with the growth of the business. The entrepreneur will add more direct employees to create the growing demands that increased sales creates. There may also be the need to add more administrative staff to handle the increasing workload that administrative functions such as sales, bookkeeping, information systems, and human resources require in a larger business. One of the challenges that arises during growth is knowing exactly when to add these new employees. When adding new employees there is a trade-off that must be considered. On the one hand, having the employees hired, trained, and ready to perform as the increase in workload comes along helps to ensure that the business is able to adequately meet increased demand. On the other hand, the business may not have enough cash flow to pay for the new employees until the increased demand has already occurred. "Employee stretching" is a bootstrapping technique that offers a solution to this dilemma.

When an entrepreneur uses employee stretching, new hiring is delayed as long as possible. Current employees are asked to carry an added workload, until the business' cash flow can support additional staff. This may include asking employees to work additional hours or to improve their productivity so they can get more work accomplished during their regular time on the job. In fact, a recent survey found that two-thirds of small-business owners ask their employees to work extra hours from time-to-time to meet temporary needs of the business.[2] The effective use of employee stretching depends on cooperation from employees, which requires open and honest communication of what is being asked and why the entrepreneur needs to ask the employees to "stretch." It should be noted that employee stretching works better in certain industries and within certain job markets. For example, in situations where workers have many job opportunities, they might be less willing to engage in employee stretching for very long—or at all—if other jobs are readily available.

There are several steps that can make employee stretching effective:

- *Set an example.* Entrepreneurs should not ask employees to stretch if they are not willing to do more than their fair share. Many entrepreneurs serve as their own bookkeeper, receptionist, sales person, and janitor. When employees see the business owner being a positive and enthusiastic role model of stretching, it can be a little easier for them to be willing to do their part.

- *Set expectations.* Every newly hired employee should understand that stretching is occasionally a part of working in the company. Explain that it is a growing business and that stretching is the most effective means of assuring the financial health of the business as it grows.

- *Hire generalists.* In addition to setting expectations, it is important to hire employees who are able to perform a variety of tasks. For example, rather than hire a person who only has experience in payroll administration, hire someone who has experience with payroll, general bookkeeping, accounts payable, and accounts receivable. This kind of flexibility makes stretching more feasible and realistic.

- *Spread the burden.* Spread additional workload or tasks among several employees. Having each employee contribute a small bit of stretching reduces the impact on each individual employee.

- *Set clear time frames.* Asking employees to stretch should always be a temporary solution. Set specific milestones so everyone is clear on when new staff will be hired. The trigger for hiring new staff can be tied to units of sales, total revenue targets, or cash flow.

- *Keep promises.* When promising relief for employees who stretch it is essential that promises are kept. For example, if the entrepreneur commits to hiring another employee when excess cash flow reaches a certain amount, then the entrepreneur should follow through on this promise. Not only is this the ethical approach, but the ability to ask employees to willingly stretch again sometime in the future will depend on the entrepreneur's credibility built up through past periods of stretching.

- *Offer additional perks as thanks.* When new staff are brought on board, it is advisable to offer extra time off or some other meaningful perk to all of the employees who have been carrying the extra workload.

TIMING OF HIRING

An important part of bootstrapping as it was defined in Chapter 1 is to optimize available cash flow. Box 4-1 illustrates how Nicholas Holland used careful timing of each new hire in his business to help bootstrap his start-up Web development company. Carefully tying cash flow to the timing of each new hire allowed Nicholas to grow his business without adding additional debt or equity financing. No new employee was hired until he had enough excess cash flow to fully cover the new employee's salary and benefits for three full months.

Using the timing of hiring to help bootstrap requires that the entrepreneur develop accurate cash flow forecasts and staffing plans. Just because the business

---

BOX 4-1   START-UPS ON A SHOESTRING

Timing of New Hires

"I have what seems to be a relatively unique process for hiring people. I always want to make sure I have three months of operating funds in the bank. By month four, I knew I was going to need to hire an employee. The interesting thing was I was terrified. I thought, "I am not paying myself and I am about to hire the first person." I sat down and thought how I could be conservative and be realistic. I waited until I had three times the monthly pay needed for the new hire. I am guessing I can sell enough business in three months to make it work. This gives my employees enough time to train and get used to our business. I wait until three months cash is in the bank before I hire another employee. I am one of the lowest paid employees of the company. I pay myself a modest salary so that most of the money is left to grow the business."

(Nicholas Holland, Founder, CentreSource)

has enough cash flow in a given month does not necessarily mean that it will have the sustainable and reliable cash flow needed to fund a new position. Accurate historic cash flow statements should be used to develop a twelve-month forecast of future cash flow. Factors such as the seasonality of cash flow from revenues and expenses that are paid quarterly or annually be factored into the hiring decision. Looking at historic cash flow can help develop a more accurate assessment of true future anticipated cash flow, which will increase confidence that the business will have enough excess cash each month for the new employee(s) even when monthly variations are taken into account.

The timing of hiring also depends upon a carefully developed staffing plan. A staffing plan creates a model that ties the need for new employees to growth in sales. It helps the entrepreneur determine the priorities for new hires and the critical points at which each new position should be created and filled. The staffing plan should take into account both direct employees who are part of making the product or providing the service of the business as well as any additional administrative staff. Of course, any staffing plan should factor in all employee stretching that can be used to help bootstrap employee costs during growth.

For example, assume that a landscape contractor uses teams of three employees for each job. Each team can routinely handle twenty jobs per week, but can "stretch" for short periods of time and handle as many as twenty-five jobs per week. Because it takes time to hire and train new employees, the owner begins the hiring process when any of the teams reaches twenty jobs. He knows they can stretch for a short time and do a few extra jobs until the new employees are ready to go to work. Each supervisor can routinely manage five teams of workers. Again, these supervisors can stretch for short periods of time. When all of the supervisors have five teams working for them, the owner begins recruiting and then training a new supervisor. Each of his office staff can provide the administrative support for up to four supervisors, so each time the business adds four more supervisors, the owner must also hire another office staff person to support them with accounts receivable management, bookkeeping, and basic payroll record keeping. Finally, although the owner has done all of the sales for new clients, he knows that when the business reaches fifty teams he will need to add his first full-time sales person to help bring in new business and free his time for more general administrative and executive functions. This model provides a basic staffing plan for the owner of the landscaping business to follow.

There will be times when the needs of the staffing plan cannot be met due to limited cash flow. In these situations, the entrepreneur must rely on priorities to determine which position will be added. In our landscaping example, let's assume that when the staffing plan calls for adding another supervisor and fifteen new workers to fill the new teams, a new administrative staff person and an additional sales person are hired. But, the entrepreneur knows from the cash forecast that he cannot afford that many new employees at once. Because the business cannot grow without employees working in teams for new clients, the owner has set his top hiring priority to always be employees working directly for the customers.

Since these workers need careful supervision to ensure that work always meets his high standards for quality, his second priority will be to hire a supervisor as soon as cash flow allows. And since growth is his main priority, the sales person will be the third priority. Finally, when all other positions are filled and bringing in new revenues and the cash flows that follow, he will add the administrative staff person. This may mean that he has to cover some administrative functions himself to help keep things running.

Another method of smoothing out the transition of new employees that can sometimes be used is to bring on new hires part-time until there is enough work and adequate cash flow to support making them full-time employees. In addition to saving salary costs, this approach can postpone the additional benefit costs that are tied to full-time employment. As with the other methods of bootstrapping employee expenses that are tied to cash flow, this approach requires clear and honest communication, realistic milestones for conversion to full-time, and consistent follow-through on all commitments. Even some executive-level employees can be hired on a part-time basis. For example, after we sold our healthcare business, I served as a part-time CEO to a couple of start-up healthcare companies that could not afford, and really didn't need a full-time executive leader. This arrangement worked out quite well for the start-up, providing them with part-time, experienced management talent until the business grew large enough to hire a full-time CEO. I was able to help in the recruiting and selection of the permanent, full-time CEO.

THE VIRTUAL TEAM

The widespread use of the Internet has allowed for the proliferation of the use of what are known as virtual teams. A *virtual team* is a group that "operates virtually, without the physical limitations of distance, time, and organizational boundaries."[3] A virtual team takes the concept of a virtual office discussed in Chapter 3 one step further. The use of virtual teams allows entrepreneurs to bootstrap by only engaging people with specific skills *only when they are needed*. In some cases, these people may be located anywhere in the world. As the definition implies, the virtual team is often made up of people who do not work in the same organization. The team comes together to work on a specific project and then disperses. So in addition to only paying for their contribution to a specific project, the entrepreneur is not responsible for payroll costs or benefits. Outsourcing and the use of independent contractors are at the heart of creating virtual teams. These topics will be discussed in detail in Chapter 5.

Dr. Jim Stefansic considers his former professors from his MBA program and other experienced entrepreneurs from the community who took an interest in the business he co-founded to be part of his virtual team. "I have access to the experts who have more experience and I was able to use my advisors and professors to check over business plans to get advice and experience. They were free consultants."

EMPLOYEE LEASING AND TEMPORARY EMPLOYEES

Entrepreneurs can reduce employment costs by subcontracting with firms that provide employees for short-term needs through employee leasing or temporary employment contracts. This avoids the problems that can arise by hiring permanent employees for what are really only short-term workload needs. Using such firms can also keep administrative overhead lower, as these firms perform all of the human resources functions for these employees. Employees of all levels of skills and experience are available on a temporary basis—even executive-level employees can be hired on a temporary basis through such arrangements. Small companies can gain the expertise of a part-time, temporary chief executive officer, chief financial officer, operations manager, controller, and so forth to help navigate through a specific, complex issue or a particularly difficult time in the company's growth. Here are some tips on finding part-time executive talent:

- Find placement firms specialize in recruiting and placing part-time executive help.
- Network within your industry to identify people willing to serve in such a role.
- Network within the local business community, through professionals such as attorneys and CPAs, or through business groups such as the Chamber of Commerce.
- Contact consulting firms that offer such services under longer-term arrangements.

USING STUDENT INTERNS

Hiring student interns is a means to hire often well-trained workers at a relatively inexpensive cost. High school students may wish to gain more significant work experience than they can get through typical fast food and retail jobs. Such work often can help them explore possible career paths that they may wish to pursue after graduation or in college. University students, both undergraduate and graduate, are eager to work as interns in business so they can list such work experience on their resumes. Smaller businesses are beginning to take advantage of this pool of workers that in the past was mainly used by large corporations. Student interns are willing to work for relatively low pay in exchange for the experience that can be gained by such work. In some cases, the interns may work for no pay if they are gaining college credit for their experience. Beyond any direct cost savings, there are several additional benefits from hiring student interns:[4]

- ***Good employees.*** Because they want to get a strong reference from their internship experience and may even have hopes of being hired full time in the future, interns are hard-working, reliable employees.

- *Flexibility.* They are willing to perform a wide variety of tasks, which allows them to be used to fill in as needed in key areas.

- *Good for morale.* Having enthusiastic young workers around can help rejuvenate the workforce.

- *Employee benefit.* Employees benefit from interns as they can cover people's jobs during summer vacations. Many companies also give priority to the children of current employees as interns.

NONSALARY COMPENSATION

On average, entrepreneurs pay about 90 percent of what larger employers pay for comparable employees.[5] So how can entrepreneurs attract the kind of talent they need when they cannot match the salaries offered by larger employers? Entrepreneurs are able to attract employees with lower salaries by offering various nonsalary compensation programs and what are known as "soft perks," which are benefits that do require the use of any of the business's precious cash flow. Nonmonetary soft perks help bootstrap a business by allowing the entrepreneur to offer things other than salary and typical benefits, which reduce the total employment costs for the business.

Just the chance to be part of entrepreneurial venture can be a soft perk that many potential employees will value highly. People typically view working in entrepreneurial ventures as a positive place to work. The challenge and excitement of being part of a growing, entrepreneurial venture can help to attract talented managers and workers seeking this type of work environment. Entrepreneurial ventures can offer challenging and more interesting work. For example, rather than just filling a specific position in a marketing department of a large company that has a narrow set of tasks and limited responsibility, the employee in an entrepreneurial venture might actually *be* the marketing department. Such a position offers a wide variety of tasks and significant responsibilities. Many employees report that management jobs in small businesses are more fulfilling and rewarding due to the high level of control and responsibility that they often carry. If the company is growing, such a position offers the opportunity to help build the company and develop systems, structures, and processes to facilitate growth. All of these characteristics of working in an entrepreneurial venture can foster professional growth.

Small businesses and entrepreneurial ventures also have the ability to offer flexibility and meet specific employee's needs. Offering flexibility for employees is a form of bootstrapping as it does not require the direct expenditure of cash. However, employees may highly value flexibility. Smaller companies can offer more flexibility, as they usually have not developed a large number of formalized policies that define every aspect of employment that are typically in place in larger businesses. Flexibility can be centered on hours worked, work schedules, and even days off. The one caution is to avoid any flexible arrangements that disrupt perceived equity between employees. The perception that compensation is relatively fair from employee to employee is critical for morale and performance.

One entrepreneur offered this story to illustrate how he used the soft perks of working in an entrepreneurial venture to attract a key employee:

> There was a manager I wanted to hire to run a new program we were starting, as he was one of the best in our industry. He worked for a large, national company. I knew I could not match his salary, but I did not give up. I got to know him and found out what he was really looking for in his career and in a job. He wanted to have more control over his department. That was easy as we were small and our structure was quite decentralized. He could run the new program like it was his own business.
>
> There was one more thing he wanted, however, and it was clear it was a deal breaker for him. His current employer had very strict rules on vacations and holidays. He was a Viet Nam veteran and had wanted to go to Washington, DC each Veterans Day to remember his fallen comrades. His current employer's rules did not make it possible to guarantee that, and he had missed the last two Veterans Day observances. So, in my offer I promised him that he would be guaranteed Veterans Day and one work day on either side of it off each and every year (they were counted as vacation days). That was all it took to convince him that we were the best place for him to work. He came to work for us taking a significant cut in base salary from what he had been making before.

The culture of an entrepreneurial venture or other smaller companies can also be a soft perk that attracts employees. Entrepreneurs build company cultures that are based on a sense of "family" and are based on having fun. There a lots of ways to let loose, have fun, and build camaraderie. Bowling outings, golf tournaments, softball teams, setting up a basketball hoop in the parking lot, talent contests are just a few of the other activities that small-business owners have used effectively. Building a good company culture is a powerful tool to not only attract employees, but retain them as well. It is not all about the money for employees. They also want a good place to work.

OTHER COMPENSATION AND BENEFITS

In addition to salary and soft perks, there are other forms of compensation that can be tied to the performance of the business. This is a form of bootstrapping that optimizes cash flow in the business. The various forms of compensation in this section are tied to the ability of the business to pay out the compensation through improved cash flow.

PROFIT SHARING

Profit-sharing programs share the profits earned by a business with employees, typically on an annual or sometimes quarterly basis. Profit sharing can be part of a formal plan that designates a predetermined amount that will be paid out to each eligible employee. In small businesses, profit sharing is often informal. Each year the owner(s) determine what portion of the profit they intend to distribute to employees and create a pool of funds for this compensation. The amount each employee receives may be tied to specific criteria such as longevity with the business, annual performance, and contribution to the overall performance of the company. Profit-sharing programs range from those that only compensate selected management employees to programs that share a portion of the profits with all employees in the company. A survey by the National Federation of Independent Businesses found that fifty-two percent of small-business owners said that they paid employees periodic bonuses or profit-sharing based on the performance of the business. In this same survey, 70 percent of small businesses offer profit-sharing programs to all employees.[6]

EQUITY COMPENSATION

Employees may be willing to work for less salary now with the hope of earning much more through directly sharing in future profits or in the proceeds of a business sale or taking a business public through equity compensation programs. Although employees who join the company near the time of the initial start-up may be issued actual stock in the new company in place of a higher market salary, there are clear disadvantages to issuing equity outright to employees. Owning stock in the business makes these employees shareholders with all of the rights that come with ownership. There are six disadvantages to carefully weigh when considering issuing stock directly to employees:

- Issuing stock or other form of ownership to employees dilutes the founders' share of future profits and wealth generated by the business. Employees with stock will have the right to a share of profit distributions to owners and to proceeds from the sale of the business if that becomes the exit event for the founders sometime in the future.

- Issuing stock to employees can create "nuisance stockholders." Minority stockholders (those owning a small percentage of the business) have specific protection under most state laws. They cannot simply be out-voted by the founders on every issue. They are afforded specific rights when it comes to decisions related to selling, merging, or restructuring the ownership of the corporation. Although they cannot block such transactions, they can complicate them to the point that a potential suitor or investor may choose to walk away. Motivations for disrupting such transactions can include concern over long-term employment under new ownership, revenge, if the employee is disgruntled, or in some cases greed (hoping to hold out support for additional payments).

- The ownership in a business and the long-term benefits it can create is simply not a tangible motivator for some employees.

- Adding additional owners increases the cost of maintaining the corporate entity, specifically tax compliance and legal costs.

- Ownership can be easily misunderstood by some employees. Ownership and employment are legally distinct roles. Those who are owners only officially act on issues at formally called stockholder or partnership meetings. Employees who have ownership in the business may falsely believe that owning stock may afford them special rights even when acting in their role as employee.

- A larger number of owners can increase the litigation risk for a business. There has been an increase in ownership related lawsuits over the past decades.

Stock options are another vehicle for employee equity compensation. With stock options the employees have the right to purchase a set number of shares of stock in the company at a predetermined price (usually at a slight discount of the value of the shares when the stock is issued). If the company becomes highly profitable the employee can purchase the stock (known as exercising their option) and receive the benefits of those profits. Or, if the business is sold, the employee can purchase the stock at the discounted price and immediately sell it as the business is sold. Stock options require a formal plan that details the guidelines for any employee who participates in the plan. There are also standardized agreements that each employee participant signs that define the strike price (predetermined purchase price), number of shares represented by the option, and the time limit of the option (options expire at a predetermined date). Many employers tie options to the specific performance of the employee or to the performance of the business. It is ethical for the company to provide clear information on tax issues that may arise for the employee and to recommend that they seek independent advice from an attorney and/or tax accountant.

EQUITY-LIKE COMPENSATION

Phantom stock and *stock appreciation rights* (SAR) are bonus compensation plans for employees where the employee does not actually receive stock or the promise of stock through options. Instead, the employee is given a written promise of a bonus that is calculated as if they did own a certain number of shares of stock. With these plans employees get the economic advantages as if they owned stock, without the complexities of actual stock ownership. Employers do not have to give up actual equity and add additional shareholders, while at the same time employees in these plans get all the financial benefits that would have come with owning actual stock. As such, many entrepreneurs view these plans as a win-win for the entrepreneur and the employees. Under phantom stock and SAR plans, employees receive a periodic bonus based on the growth in the value of the business using a predetermined model for valuation. Employees are taxed when they receive the bonus at the same rate as ordinary income. Since they do not actually own any equity or stock in the business, they are not eligible for lower capital gains tax rates.

Entrepreneurs who use these plans should establish in advance a total amount that will be issued through these bonuses. For example, when setting up a phantom stock plan the entrepreneur decides that he or she will issue phantom stock bonuses that are the equivalent of having his or her employees own 20 percent of his or her business. Once that pool is established, he or she should manage that total amount prudently so he or she can offer new employees this bonus plan and/or increase bonuses for employees whose performance merits a larger bonus.

Because there are tax and legal issues that can arise with these plans, they should be set up carefully with the help of experienced tax and legal experts. If the bonuses are set aside, cash should be put into a special trust to avoid possible tax issues for employee. Also, there are possible ERISA (Employee Retirement Income Security Act of 1974) issues that may arise with these plans if they are not structured properly.

The final component of the total employee compensation package includes benefits, such as paid vacations, employee discounts, health insurance, and retirement plans. Offering these benefits can be a particular challenge for start-ups due to limited resources and tight cash flow. But for many employees, these benefits are an expectation of employment. Bootstrapping strategies related to this part of employee compensation are often required for an entrepreneur to be able to afford standard employee benefits and compete with larger employers for these workers.

Paid Vacations

The most common employee benefit small-business owners offer to employees is paid time off—75 percent offer paid vacations and 59 percent offer paid sick leave. Vacation time and sick days are likely to be an expected benefit by many employees. Although paid time off is a cost due to lost productivity during the time that employees are not at work, a bootstrapping entrepreneur can manage the cash flow implications of this benefit. The entrepreneur can set policies that restrict time vacation time to periods of lower demand. The impact of vacations on productivity can also be mitigated by ensuring that employees do not all take days off during the same time periods by requiring that all vacation time be preapproved. Priority for more popular time off can be given to employees based on seniority of employment or as a bonus for superior performance.[7]

Employee Discounts

Fifty-four percent of entrepreneurs provide discounted or free goods or services from the business to their employees as a benefit.[8] For example, a restaurant may offer free or discounted meals to workers, while a clothing store may offer merchandise at cost to employees. Many employees perceive this type of benefit to have an even greater value than the actual cost to the employer, thus making it a form of bootstrapping.

EMPLOYER-SPONSORED HEALTH INSURANCE

A recent survey of small-business owners found that 47 percent offer health plans to their employees (fewer offer disability, life, and dental insurance).[9] The cost of offering health insurance has increased dramatically over the past several years. Several states have begun to require employee health insurance plans for even small employers. Other states are passing legislation that allows small employers to enter into cooperative buying groups to help bring together their employees into a larger pool that can help bring down the cost of health insurance. Since employee-sponsored health insurance is an expectation of most skilled workers or in some cases required by law, smaller employers must increasingly be prepared to offer this benefit to attract and retain the employees they need for their businesses.

One approach to keeping health insurance costs lower is to annually shop for lower rates from other insurance carriers. Insurance providers will often use pricing as a means to attract new business. Rates can be increased once a year, so insurance carriers will often increase premiums after the first year of coverage. Shopping for lower rates each year can be time consuming, but many employers find that doing so can dramatically decrease the cost of health insurance. An independent insurance broker may be able to assist the employer in searching for lower rates. Since they are paid by the insurance carriers, this service does not directly cost the entrepreneur. Internet searches can also be an effective approach to shopping for insurance policies.

A challenge that small employers face is that they bring a small pool of employees to the health insurance carrier. Rates are based on the pool of people covered under a policy—the larger the pool of employees the lower the rate since any individuals with higher health care costs are spread over more covered lives. Therefore, small employers will almost always pay higher rate than large employers due to the higher risk faced with a smaller number of employees. And if a small employer has even one or two employees with high health care costs due to serious illnesses, the rates can become unaffordable.

One alternative practice that many small-business owners are choosing as a means of helping employees get health insurance is to encourage them to buy their own policy and then get reimbursed by the business. Some employers to utilize a program called Health Reimbursement Arrangement (HRA). This type of plan works like a health savings account that is used by many large employers. Under an HRA plan, employers can set aside a certain sum every month that employees can use for health expenses including the purchase of an individual health insurance policy. The employer can expense this set-aside just like traditional health benefits, and the money does not count as taxable income for the employee. Because individual health insurance policies are often put into larger pools they can often end up being much less expensive than a small employer policy. One shortcoming of this approach is that it can be difficult for employees with preexisting conditions to purchase affordable coverage. Also, there are questions being raised about the legality of this approach to helping employees get health insurance coverage in some states.

EMPLOYEE TRAINING

A part of the expense of adding new employees is the cost of training and the time it takes for a new worker to become fully productive. Employee training is also a cost for existing employees, as new methods or new equipment may be implemented to improve productivity or increase performance. Training costs can be bootstrapped by taking advantage of published training materials, online training programs, or publically available classes, all of which are generally much less expensive than developing such programs in-house. For example, there are a variety of off-the-shelf training materials and online tutorials for most of the commonly used software programs.

Another bootstrapping principle associated with training relates to employee development. A growing entrepreneurial business will need to add more management staff. It is almost always less expensive to develop management talent from current employees than it is to hire from the outside. For example, a growing small business may offer training and education opportunities to a bookkeeper so that at the point that the business needs a controller, that employee will be prepared to take on that added responsibility. Another example would be paying for basic supervisory training courses to hourly workers so they can become prepared to be team leaders or supervisors as the business grows.

PAYROLL COSTS

Due to the complexity of the income tax system, there is a cost to complying with all of the legal requirements associated paying employees and filing all of the mandated forms and reports. The Small Business Administration estimates that the cost of income tax compliance for small employers averages $1,200 per year per employee. Much of this cost is associated with the expense of employing staff to process payroll and file all of the required forms and reports. A practice that can help to reduce the cost associated with paying employees is to outsource the processing of payroll to an outside vendor. Because of the efficiency of their payrolls systems, these vendors can process payroll at a fraction of the cost of employing a payroll specialist. Small businesses that process their own payrolls can run into trouble with the Internal Revenue Service (IRS) due to late or improperly filed payroll tax deposits and required tax forms. Using an outside payroll vendor helps ensure the accuracy and timeliness of all required income tax payments and filings required by the IRS.

One disadvantage of outsourcing to a payroll service is that they automatically withdraw funds for payroll and tax deposits from the employer's checking account a day or two in advance of each disbursement. This eliminates any flexibility that the entrepreneur may need from time to time with the timing of payroll. Such flexibility is a part of bootstrapping for many entrepreneurs as it relates to the timing of cash flow. For example, when cash flow is tight small businesses often delay the paychecks of the owners, and if necessary even their managers. This is not possible when using a payroll service.

Conclusion and Summary

This chapter examined the bootstrapping opportunities for the various costs associated with employees. For many entrepreneurial ventures, employee costs can be the largest single category of expense. Bootstrapping techniques discussed included those related to employee compensation, the use of temporary employees and interns, nonsalary compensation and benefits, employee training, and payroll expenses.

Chapter 5 will explore bootstrapping techniques that can help bring down the total cost associated with making a product or providing a service through the creation of more efficient systems and processes in the business.

Discussion Questions

1. How can an entrepreneur bootstrap the costs associated with existing employees?
2. Discuss how the use of virtual teams, temporary employees, and student interns can help bootstrap employee costs.
3. Describe how the various categories of nonsalary employee compensation and benefits can be bootstrapped.
4. The indirect costs of having employees associated with employee training and payroll expenses offer opportunities to bootstrap. Explain using specific examples.

Endnotes

1. http://www.nfib.com/object/sbPolls.
2. Ibid.
3. Duarte, D. and Snyder, N. (2006). *Mastering Virtual Teams: Strategies, Tools, and Techniques that Succeed*. San Francisco: Jossey-Bass, p. 4.
4. Gangemi, R. (1995). Interns: More than You Bargained For. *Inc.com*. Retrieved on January 4, 2008 from http://www.inc.com/magazine/19950201/2155.html.
5. http://www.sba.gov/advo/research/.
6. http://www.nfib.com/object/sbPolls.
7. Ibid.
8. Ibid.
9. Ibid.

CHAPTER 5

BOOTSTRAPPING THROUGH EFFICIENT PROCESSES

Buschman had little money, but he was clever with machinery. Keeping his regular job—and using $500 in overtime pay—he scrounged in junkyards for materials to construct a little factory in his basement. "There's a feeling you need tons of money and bank financing . . . to start a business . . . . If I needed a tow motor, I'd find something at a junkyard, change the engine and transmission, and rebuild it."[1]

Overview

Outsourcing

Efficient Manufacturing

Inventory Management

Conclusion and Summary

LEARNING OBJECTIVES

- ✓ Understand the various opportunities to use outsourcing for businesses of all types and all stages of development
- ✓ Recognize how to create more efficient processes in a manufacturing business to facilitate bootstrapping
- ✓ Explain how proper inventory management can help bootstrapping by preserving cash flow
- ✓ Apply these bootstrapping principles to an actual or planned business venture

OVERVIEW

This chapter begins by examining how bootstrapping can be achieved in small businesses and high growth ventures by creating more efficient processes. Outsourcing has become a common means to create efficiency for businesses of all sizes. Outsourcing techniques can be used by businesses producing products and services.[2] Outsourcing can also incorporate entire components of a business, such as manufacturing and distribution, to specific tasks through subcontracting. Bootstrapping can help manufacturing entities through cost-saving techniques that reduce the cost of both equipment and facilities. Techniques creating more efficient systems can bootstrap by helping to preserve cash. It is important to remember that cash is a scarce resource for most businesses at any stage of development. Finally, this chapter will show how bootstrapping can include various inventory-management techniques that reduce the amount of cash a firm requires to maintain raw material and finished-goods inventories.

OUTSOURCING

When starting a new venture a common bootstrapping strategy is to outsource the actual production of the product.[3] *Outsourcing*, also known as *subcontracting*, is when a business enters into a formal agreement to have another company that has the capacity, equipment and expertise, perform part or all of the actual production process.

At first it may not appear that outsourcing is truly a bootstrapping strategy. After all, the company that is contracted to outsource will need to add in their own profit margin on any part of the production process that they perform. However, there are three reasons outsourcing can actually be a very effective means of bootstrapping.

First, starting a business that produces a product can be quite expensive. The start-up costs will include the costs of securing the space and equipment needed to make a product. The cost to buy a building and equipment can easily run into the hundreds of thousands or even millions of dollars. In some cases it may be possible to lease space and equipment. But whether the entrepreneur finances the purchase of a building and equipment or is able to lease them, in either case there will be an immediate and often significant increase in the business's overhead expenses. As discussed in Chapter 2, increased overhead leads to a higher level of revenues required to reach breakeven. The start-up costs will also include paying for all of the employees needed to produce the product. Because there is a time lag between when a product is produced and when the product is actually purchased and paid for, the entrepreneur will need to have enough funding to cover the initial employee costs to begin production and build up enough inventory to sell. There are actually two types of inventory costs that will need to be paid for out of the start-up budget—the initial raw material inventory and the finished goods inventory that needs to be on hand to fill customer orders.

Second, by contracting with a company that already has production processes in place, the entrepreneur can often obtain lower per unit prices than if he or she were to try and produce the firm's product. The established company has likely already set up efficient processes and has created an economy of scale that keeps per-unit prices lower. The established company has made it through the initial learning curve that can create higher prices for a start-up business. A higher volume of production helps drive down the cost per unit as the system reaches its optimum capacity. In turn, reaching this point allows a firm to spread out its overhead costs on the maximum number of units. Also, in many situations the company contracted for outsourcing is able to buy raw materials at a lower cost per unit because of the volume of its production and the favorable pricing it can achieve due to its economic power in purchasing.

Finally, local economic conditions may create lower cost structures for companies that operate in that region. Certain regions within the United States have lower wage rates that can reduce costs. Such cost savings can be even more dramatic when production is outsourced to many foreign companies. With increased globalization, international outsourcing has become fairly common even for small businesses and entrepreneurial ventures. In fact, these types of firms are finding sources in China, India, Mexico, Indonesia, the Caribbean, Eastern Europe, and Russia, to name just a few. Some firms in countries such as these can offer much lower labor and material costs that can more than offset the added cost of shipping from such geographic distances.

Businesses that sell physical products often seek to find suppliers in other countries to help reduce the cost of production. This type of outsourcing is known as *low-cost country sourcing*, which can range from the production of component parts that are shipped to the United States for assembly, to the complete production of the product by a foreign source. Although low-cost country sourcing can result in significant savings, care must be taken to understand the actual cost of outsourcing production in this manner.

Nuvar is a high growth assembling, thermoforming, and engineering company located in Holland, Michigan that uses outsourcing to help fuel its growth. Mark Kuyper, President of Nuvar, cautions that entrepreneurs should understand the actual cost of outsourcing a product through low-cost countries. "The costs associated with ordering components, shipping components, warehousing components, monitoring quality of the components, traveling to Asia are all costs that must be considered." Even with all of these costs factored in, outsourcing can save 10–20 percent over the cost of manufacturing products in the United States. Nuvar plans each outsourced product using a "mini business plan" to ensure that they have taken all costs into account and planned for all logistical challenges. Kuyper has found that successful outsourcing takes a significant amount of his time. Outsourcing is a growing practice worldwide, including businesses outside the United States looking for outsourcing opportunities around the globe including using businesses within the United States (Table 5-1).

Although outsourcing has historically been associated primarily with manufactured products, more small technology firms are also relying on outsourcing to

TABLE 5-1 Opportunities for Bootstrapping Production	
Stage of Production Process	*Description*
Product development	Includes research and development, prototyping and intellectual property protection.
	Examples: European Internet telephony company Skype and the music-sharing business Kazaa both outsourced to developers in Estonia to develop these products.
Production	The most common form of outsourcing involves production or manufacturing. Primary source of savings is the lower cost of labor.
	Examples: China, India, Mexico, Viet Nam, Taiwan are all major producers of goods made for U.S. businesses of all sizes due to lower labor costs they can offer.
Assembly and installation	Certain stages of assembly or installation can often be outsourced to vendors with more expertise in that specific phase of the process and more efficient operations.
	Example: Softub, a medium spa manufacturer in California, contracted out the assembly of the motor, pump, and the control unit for their hot tubs to allow them to focus on sales and product development.*
Packaging and shipping	Even if the entrepreneur makes the product, it may be advantageous to outsource the packaging of the finished goods to assure professional looking packaging that will protect the product during distribution. Many vendors also can provide order fulfillment, including shipping and delivery.
	Example: Many home-based e-commerce businesses are able to achieve significant scale by outsourcing not only packaging and shipping, but also inventory management.

* http://www.inc.com/tools/1999/10/13784.html, retrieved on March 25, 2008.

develop software and other information technology products. Highly skilled technology workers can be found around the globe and the speed of the Internet has helped make collaboration and communication relatively easy. The advantages of outsourcing information technology include cost savings, access to more current knowledge and skills, and access to increased capacity for data storage and servers. In an example presented in Chapter 2, Andy Tabar, founder of the Web development company Bizooki, has established partnerships with developers in India whom he can call on as needed to help work on large projects. For about the cost of hiring inexperienced developers in the United States, Tabar is able to tap into developers in India who were trained in the United States and also have years of Web development experience.

Pursuing outsourcing agreements requires careful planning and formal written contracts that clearly define the work being performed by the outsourced company. The contract should address a number of issues, such as the following:

- a specific definition of the scope of the work to be performed
- explicit deadlines and timelines

- payment terms and conditions, including agreed upon currency rates for foreign contracts
- consequences for nonperformance

For manufacturing outsourcing, the contracts should include quality and other performance expectations and specifications, including any raw materials used in the production process. When evaluating outsourcing alternatives, firms to whom the venture might outsource should be fully vetted. Careful vetting includes actions such as checking references carefully and evaluating the firms' specific experiences with the type of work to be performed. Although price (or cost) is a major consideration in outsourcing, it should not be the only criterion in making a final choice.

There are additional considerations when outsourcing with a company outside the United States. Issues such as intellectual property protection, performance expectations, and communication are examples. We will examine these types of issues in greater detail:[4]

- *Learn the culture.* Business practices, language and terminology, and ethical standards vary widely around the globe. It is important to not only understand what the source company will be doing, but *how* that company will perform the work within the local culture. Any source used will be considered an extension of the company. Many businesses have had adverse public relations because of the practices of their foreign suppliers. This can include labor practices, such as child labor that is permissible and even common in some countries. Other practices, such as poor quality control of materials used that result in products that are not up to U.S. standards can also create serious and even catastrophic problems. Recent examples from China, including poisonous materials added to dog food as filler and lead paint used on children's toys, have driven some small companies in the United States out of business because of the cost of recalling the products and cancelled orders.

- *Take steps to protect intellectual property.* Just because an entrepreneur has a U.S. patent does not mean that he or she will have strong intellectual property protection in other countries. One critical step is to find a source that is not already a direct competitor for the entrepreneur's product. It is also advisable to break-up the production over several different companies—have each company responsible for completing a single step in the manufacturing process. These actions help ensure that no one company can obtain all of the intellectual property of the product and its production.

- *Determine the total cost and turnaround for delivery.* It is advisable to talk to other U.S.-based companies that have used the source to get an understanding of all of the costs associated with outsourcing and the realistic timing of deliveries. It is also important to fully evaluate the time and cost of various shipping options, as both can vary widely. Countries that are low-cost manufacturers today may not be the lowest cost options in the future. Exchange rates, new tax structures, changing government policies and economic strategies, and increasing labor costs can increase costs over time. For example, many companies that outsource are beginning to shift their partnerships from countries like China to firms in other nations—such as Mexico, Viet Nam and India—where costs are even lower.

- *Provide a working prototype for the product.* Any prototype should be made of the exact materials and components that are defined in the specifications of the contract. Since grades of materials can vary, this should also be made explicit. Quality is cited as one of the biggest challenges of outsourcing.

- *Communicate frequently and openly with the source.* This may help minimize surprises. Generally, foreign sources do not initiate communication if there are any problems. "I'm not sure any reasonable volume of importing would be possible without e-mail," says Mark Kuyper of Nuvar. In addition to Internet communication, face-to-face visits to sources on a regular basis are a common practice. Once a year is the minimum; but, some outsourcing companies are visited as frequently as once a month. Relationships are very important in many cultures, and face-to-face meetings are viewed as the only true way to get to know business partners.

Potential outsourcing partners are typically identified through referrals, contacts at trade shows, and organizations that specialize in linking U.S. companies with foreign producers.

Outsourcing does not always involve contracting with another company. Working with individuals, known as *independent contractors*, is outsourcing work to individuals within the United States, which is governed by federal employee laws. Many smaller companies use independent contractors to keep employee expenses lower. Independent contractors are engaged for specific projects, so there are only costs to the company hiring them when there is specific work to be performed. In addition, independent contractors do not have to be covered under workers' compensation insurance or other employee benefits, and the company does not have to pay the employer portion of Social Security and Medicare taxes.

However, the IRS and the courts have established strict guidelines on who can be considered a true independent contractor in recent years. This has come in large part because of employers who used the status of independent contractor for people who were really employees simply to reduce their costs by saving on benefit costs and the expense associated with the employer Social Security match. The status of independent contractor versus employee is not guided by a specific law, but by a series of court cases. There is no simple checklist, but rather a growing list of criteria that help determine independent contractor status. Therefore, a certified public accountant or an attorney should be consulted to help assure that a business with whom the entrepreneur is thinking about forming a working relationship is in compliance with the current interpretation of this area of tax law.

According to the IRS, "A general rule is that you, the payer, have the *right to control or direct only the result of the work* done by an independent contractor, and *not the means and methods of accomplishing the result*."[5] Additional guidelines regarding who can be considered an independent contractor versus an employee are as follows:[6]

- Individuals will likely be considered employees if they receive "extensive" (note that the definition of this term is left up to interpretation by the IRS) instruction on:
  - how, when, or where to do the work they will perform
  - what tools or equipment to use
  - where to purchase supplies and services
- Individuals will likely be considered employees if they receive training about required procedures and methods.
- Individuals will likely be considered independent contractors if they:
  - make a significant investment in their work
  - are not directly reimbursed for expenses
  - have the ability to make profit or loss on their work
  - receive no benefits from the company, such as health insurance and paid vacation

In the past, the IRS would allow people to be considered independent contractors if they met some portion of these rules. But over time the IRS has become much stricter in interpreting the rules. Now it is generally considered that all of the rules must be met to classify an individual as a true independent contractor and not an employee. Written contracts between the company and the individual that clearly define the relationship using the above criteria can also help support that a person is a true independent contractor.

EFFICIENT MANUFACTURING

Even a business that begins with outsourcing may eventually decide to bring production in-house. The business may have reached a size that will create sufficient volume to make in-house production cost effective, largely by developing economies of scale. Bringing production in-house can also improve quality assurance, reduce delivery time, protect intellectual property, and allow for more rapid product changes.

For businesses that manufacture products, there are several techniques to help in bootstrapping. As discussed in Chapter 3, it is possible to realize significant savings by buying equipment through auctions, from business closings, from other businesses that have outgrown their smaller machinery, and even from salvage companies or junkyards. For example, Colonial Container, a start-up box manufacturing company, was able to find all the machinery it needed for its first two years of operation by buying equipment that another company was ready to send to salvage. This equipment was purchased at scrap metal prices of a few pennies per pound. Once the equipment had been painted and basic maintenance performed, it was in good enough condition to operate reliably for several more years. The cost of buying, transporting, and restoring this equipment was less than 20 percent of the cost of buying comparable new equipment. In addition, the company that sold the machinery allowed payment over two years with no interest.

Bootstrapping techniques can even be observed when manufacturers are building or expanding their facilities. Located in Pulaski, TN, Richland LLC is a growing company specializing in large scale industrial equipment. "When we are about to expand, we look around for other buildings we can offer to remove or demo," says company President Jim Greene. Before they demolish the building they salvage all of the materials they can, particularly all heavy steel. They then use these materials to build their own new buildings or for building expansions. They also use their own workers to provide most of the labor to build facilities, utilizing any down time they have between projects. They have been able to build new facilities through this bootstrapping technique at a savings of 70–90 percent.

Another path to bootstrapping manufacturing is through the implementation of techniques such as *lean manufacturing* and *Six Sigma*, which can help streamline processes and eliminate waste. Using lean manufacturing, waste is defined in terms of overproduction, waiting or idle time, transportation costs, over processing, high levels of inventory, excess movement, and scrap or defects. All of these are viewed as symptoms of underlying problems in the manufacturing process as it is currently designed. Six Sigma is an approach that uses data, processes, and tools to nearly eliminate defects and bring performance close to perfection.

Many small businesses and entrepreneurial ventures experience financial distress in large part because they fail to understand the basic cost of making their product. The knowledge needed to avoid this problem can come from understanding basic cost accounting. Understanding the cost of making a product or of providing a service can help the entrepreneur become more effective at setting prices that truly earn a profit for the business, can help decide what contract to pursue, and even determine what products or services should be offered to market. For example, an engineering firm had three lines of business: municipal street planning, site planning for large residential developments, and surveying. The owners were trying to determine how to grow the profitability of the business. Since the three founding partners each had expertise in one of the three lines of business, the company had historically grown these three services at a fairly even pace and assumed they would continue to do so into the future. However, when a consultant they hired asked which service was most profitable, the owners were unsure. They knew their overall profits, but did not know how much each of the services contributed to the firm's profits. The consultant then helped the owners determine the true full cost of each service. They were shocked to learn that only one of the services they provided, site planning for large residential developments, actually made money when all costs were factored in. And in fact, they actually had been losing money on each project they performed for municipal street planning. With this knowledge the owners made the decision to shift their efforts into site planning for large residential developments. Without adding any staff, the firm was able to more than double its profits by understanding the true cost of each service.

There are two types of cost accounting systems. *Job order costing* is used for businesses in which each job is fairly distinct and requires its own pricing. House painting and landscaping are both examples of businesses that use job order costing. The total cost for a job using this method includes the direct labor and materials, plus an allocation of total overhead applied to that specific job. The allocation of overhead is based on a consistent unit that applies to all jobs—quite often it is based on labor hours worked on the job. For example, assume that a landscaper has total overhead costs of $10,000 per year and that he bills out 2,000 hours in an average year. He would allocate $10,000 overhead/2,000 hours = $5 per hour worked on the job. So if a job took 10 hours, he would allocate overhead costs of $50 to that job.

The second type of cost accounting is called *process costing*. This method is used when a business makes a large number of the same product. For example, a small business that makes snowboards uses this method. Total overhead using process costing is allocated to each product. For example, assume that the snowboard company had $10,000 in total overhead costs and made 2,000 snowboards each year. This company would allocate $5 per snowboard in overhead in addition to the materials and labor it takes to make each snowboard to determine the true total cost.

In addition to using basic cost accounting to make product and pricing decisions, the technique also clearly shows the impact of overhead on the price of each job performed or each unit produced. This underscores the importance of keeping overhead low in a bootstrapping environment as discussed in previous chapters. Lower overhead allows for the entrepreneur to charge a more competitive price or to make more profit per job or per unit.

INVENTORY MANAGEMENT

Businesses that are positioned anywhere in the supply chain from manufacturing all the way to retail sales can benefit from inventory-management techniques that aid in bootstrapping. Inventories are comprised of both raw materials used to manufacture the product and finished products that are waiting to be shipped to customers, being stored in warehouses, or sitting on retailers' shelves. Poorly managed inventories can tie up large amounts of cash. The key measure of the effectiveness of inventory management is *inventory turnover*, which tells how often the inventory of a business is completely sold. The higher the inventory turnover ratio, the less cash tied up in inventory. Inventory turnover can be measured monthly or annually.

The formula for inventory turnover is:

$$\text{Inventory turnover} = \frac{\text{Cost of Goods Sold}}{\text{Average Inventory}}$$

Taking a simple example, assume an art gallery had a cost of goods sold for the previous year of $600,000 and an average inventory for the year (calculated by adding the beginning inventory for the year to the ending inventory for the year and dividing that number by two) of $50,000. The inventory turnover for this gallery would be:

$$\text{Inventory turnover} = \frac{\$600,000}{\$50,000}$$
$$= 12 \text{ times per year}$$

A second gallery has the same annual sales of $600,000, but has an average inventory of $100,000. The inventory turnover for this gallery would be:

$$\text{Inventory turnover} = \frac{\$600,000}{\$100,000}$$
$$= 6 \text{ times per year}$$

In the gallery with an inventory turnover of 12 times a year, the store sells the equivalent of its entire inventory once a month. On the other hand, the gallery that has an inventory turnover of 6 times a year sells the equivalent of its entire inventory every *two* months. The second store must tie up an extra $50,000 to support the higher level of inventory. Because managing the cash flow of the business is a key aspect of bootstrapping, inventory turnover should be carefully managed by any venture that makes and/or sells product. Inventory turnover can be increased in two ways: (1) increase the volume of sales, which increases the Cost of Goods Sold part of the formula, and (2) decrease the size of the inventory needed, which decreases the Average Inventory part of the formula. As this section is addressing bootstrapping as it relates to inventory, we will focus our attention on techniques that help decrease the size of the inventory needed.

Just-in-time is one method of inventory management. As its name implies, just-in-time inventory management has the goal of keeping on hand only inventory that is needed for the current jobs being processed, rather than keeping a larger level of inventory to accommodate any and all possible future orders. To successfully implement just-in-time, the entrepreneur must have the cooperation of suppliers (raw material inventory) so that the raw materials arrive at the time they are needed for production and from customers (finished goods inventory) to ensure product will be delivered as needed to meet demand. To accomplish this, the business must develop five key elements:

- Establish a continuous inventory update system to assure that inventories are always at the proper level to meet immediate production and shipping schedules.
- Set high standards for on-time shipping to minimize the cost of back orders and keep raw materials at proper levels.
- Track time to fill back orders from suppliers when they occur and communicate data to suppliers to facilitate improved performance.

- Track customer complaints as a percentage of orders shipped to monitor timeliness and quality of finished goods.

- Accurate knowledge of the costs associated with manufacturing each product the company makes will help insure acceptable return on investment for the cash that is invested in inventory.

Another bootstrapping technique for managing inventory is to keep the inventory for a business as simple as possible. The focus should be on the small number of items that generate the most sales. For example, after carefully analyzing its sales revenue, a printing company recognized that it was carrying colors and grades of paper that were almost never being used by the firm's customers. The company had cash tied up in this inventory. So the firm aggressively trimmed its inventory by almost 80 percent to include only the most popular colors and grades. When an unusual color or grade of paper was requested, customers were told that a special order was required. Remarkably, customers did not react negatively to the new procedures.

An inventory and supply chain management technique known as "sense and respond" uses careful attention to changing customer preferences to more closely tie inventories to customer behaviors. Rather than making annual or seasonal adjustments as is the typical approach to managing inventories and product offerings, using sense and respond techniques allows for weekly or even daily adjustments. For example:

> Sales clerks at 7-Eleven Japan are required to record the gender and estimated age of every consumer and product scan what they buy. Every week, the system combines this data with its advanced demographics research to adjust product stock and store arrangement in each of its 10,000 stores.
>
> One store rotated small boxes of milk to the front of the dairy case in the morning, as its product scans showed workers buy these; larger bottles at noon, when high school students buy; and half-gallons in the afternoon, when housewives shop.[7]

Sense and respond inventory management creates a means for continuous adjustment to react to changes in customer preferences whether it is short-term patterns as in the previous example, or longer-term fundamental changes in customer preferences.

Conclusion and Summary

This chapter examined methods of bootstrapping related to creating efficient processes. Opportunities exist to bootstrap through outsourcing, which can range from entire components of a business to specific tasks through subcontracting. Businesses that manufacture products can bootstrap through how they secure the equipment and facilities needed to manufacture their products. There are also process techniques that help bootstrap by preserving cash through more efficient systems using cost accounting tools and process control techniques. Finally, boot-strapping can include various inventory-management techniques that reduce the amount of cash that needs to be committed to maintaining inventories that are larger than needed.

Chapter 6 is the first of two chapters that examine various ways to bootstrap marketing. Chapter 6 explores how start-up businesses bootstrap marketing while Chapter 7 examines bootstrap marketing within ongoing ventures.

Discussion Questions

1. How does outsourcing help bootstrap a business? List some of the steps that a business should take to ensure success with their outsourcing initiatives.
2. What are the specific requirements for subcontracting as defined by the IRS?
3. What are some steps that manufacturing ventures can take to bootstrap their operations?
4. How does inventory management allow for bootstrapping opportunities? Explain using the formula for inventory turnover. List three approaches to bootstrapping inventories.

Endnotes

1. Finegan, J. Bootstrapping: Great companies started with less than a thousand dollars. http://www.inc.com/magazine/19950801/2363_pagen_3.html, retrieved on February 15, 2008.
2. For the remainder of this chapter it will be assumed that the term *products* refers to both products and services.
3. The *production process* refers to both manufacturing a product and providing a service.
4. Kurlantzick, Joshua (2005). *Entrepreneur.* http://www.entrepreneur.com/magazine/entrepreneur/2005/june/77826-2.html, retrieved on February 27, 2008.
5. http://www.irs.gov/businesses/small/article/0,,id=99921,00.html, retrieved on February 27, 2008.
6. http://www.irs.gov/pub/irs-pdf/p1779.pdf, retrieved on February 27, 2008.
7. http://www.inc.com/magazine/20050801/supply-chain.html, retrieved on March 26, 2008.

CHAPTER 6

BOOTSTRAP MARKETING: THE START-UP VENTURE

If I had one dollar left to spend on my business, I would spend it on marketing. (Charles Hagood, Co-Founder of The Access Group and Healthcare Performance Partners)

Overview

Entrepreneurial Marketing — Dancing with the Customer

Word of Mouth and Viral Marketing — Turning Customers into a Sales Force

Publicity

New Approaches to Internet-Based Bootstrap Marketing

Don't Forget the Basics — Simple Bootstrap Marketing Tools for New Ventures

Conclusion and Summary

LEARNING OBJECTIVES

- ✓ Understand the philosophy of bootstrapping an entrepreneurial venture
- ✓ Apply basic bootstrap marketing tools for a new venture
- ✓ Examine the role of word of mouth and how an entrepreneur can proactively enhance this approach to bootstrap marketing
- ✓ Appreciate the ethical issues of bootstrap marketing

OVERVIEW

Most of the energy of an early stage entrepreneurial venture is spent refining the product or service and attracting customers.[1] These are essential elements of the marketing function of the venture, encompassing the product, pricing, and promotion components of the marketing mix. Because the typical start-up has limited resources, developing strategies and tactics to bootstrap the marketing efforts of a new venture are essential to success during this critical time.

This chapter begins with an overview of the philosophy of entrepreneurial marketing. We follow this with an examination of a variety of common tools and tactics that can be used to apply this philosophy to start-up ventures, beginning with one of the most commonly used—word of mouth. The chapter offers a sample of some of the new bootstrapping tools (such as blogs and street teams) that are emerging as means to help the entrepreneur attract customers to the start-up venture. The chapter concludes with a discussion of what are clearly the simplest marketing tools—the business cards, brochures, signs, and Web sites.

ENTREPRENEURIAL MARKETING—DANCING WITH THE CUSTOMER

Before exploring a variety of marketing tools and techniques for start-ups, it is important to understand the philosophy that guides bootstrap marketing. Schindehutte, Morris and Pitt (2009) in another book in this Prentice-Hall Entrepreneurship Series define *entrepreneurial marketing* as "an integrative construct for conceptualizing marketing in an era of change, complexity, chaos, contradiction, and diminishing resources, and one that will manifest itself differently as companies age and grow."[2] Entrepreneurial marketing is integrative, as it can be understood as being at the heart of the entrepreneurial process. Much of the entrepreneur's activity is engaging the market and becoming a "co-active producer" of innovation with the customer. Business plans rarely play out as the entrepreneur originally envisions. Once the business launches, successful entrepreneurs understand the need for an ongoing dialogue with the customer that helps to refine and evolve the original business concept. Peter Vaill (1996) describes the world of business today as being in a state of "permanent white water" to describe the era of change, complexity, chaos, and contradiction that is part of this definition of entrepreneurial marketing.[3] In this chapter, we discuss the changes that occur as a business ages and grows by examining bootstrap marketing as it manifests itself in the start-up venture; our attention shifts to marketing in the growing venture in Chapter 7.

Jay Levinson was one of the first to capture the essence of entrepreneurial marketing in his 1983 book, *Guerrilla Marketing*. Guerrilla marketing was a term Levinson used to describe the philosophical approach behind bootstrapping the marketing function. His book soon became the marketing manual for entrepreneurs who want to be effective bootstrappers. In a 2005 article published in

Entrepreneur magazine, Levinson describes the philosophy behind guerrilla marketing as follows:

> A marketing mind-set isn't just thinking about your brochures, signs, messages or packaging. It is the way you think about how all these activities and other things work together to achieve your marketing goals. It is about tying all your activity to the mission statement of your company or organization. It is about understanding your target market—who will buy from you, and why? It is the measurement of your plan, and it is about relationships with customers and prospects.[4]

More recently, John Jantsch (2007) called the bootstrappers approach to marketing *duct tape marketing*.[5] Duct tape marketing views entrepreneurial marketing as a process and a system, not a one-time event that is comprised of simple, affordable and effective techniques. What all of these definitions of entrepreneurial marketing share is the essence of bootstrapping—achieving the maximum result with the limited resources available to the entrepreneur. But, the entrepreneur should be aware that there are disadvantages to bootstrap marketing. We present the advantages and disadvantages of bootstrap marketing in Table 6-1. When evaluating these advantages and disadvantages, the entrepreneur should recall that bootstrap marketing is "only limited by the imagination of the marketer/entrepreneur who invests time, energy and creativity—instead of money."[6] Repeatedly, evidence shows that the advantages of bootstrapping far outweigh the disadvantages. The reality is that vast majority of entrepreneurs have no choice but to bootstrap during their start-up; moreover, when effectively used, bootstrap marketing is a highly effective approach to increasing sales in a new entrepreneurial venture. Bootstrap marketing is learning to "dance with the customer" to create products and services that evolve and change within the dynamic marketplace of today's economy.

TABLE 6-1   Disadvantages and Advantages of Bootstrap Marketing

Disadvantages	*Advantages*
Takes time, energy, and creativity away from an already busy and stretched entrepreneur.	Allows the entrepreneur to achieve the most important outcome during start-up—generating sales—even in the face of very limited resources.
Some bootstrap marketing techniques have significant ethical issues that can be overlooked in the haste to bootstrap.	Helps the entrepreneur firmly establish a relationship with a niche market.
Can face stiff competition from large companies with much richer marketing budgets that can maintain a more consistent message to the market.	Allows the entrepreneur to effectively compete for customers with larger firms able to outspend the start-up business.

Source: Based on Schindehutte, M., Morris, M., and Pitt, L. (2009), *Rethinking Marketing*, Upper Saddle River, NJ: Pearson Education.

In a new venture the entrepreneur must develop the right product or service for the right customer group at the right price. That is, the entrepreneur must be effective at developing what is commonly called the marketing mix—a mix that will guide the product's entry into the marketplace. The goal of bootstrap marketing is to have the same desired impact on customers as a more traditional approach to marketing used by much larger corporations—to get the customer to buy a product or service and to benefit from using the product's or the service's features. With bootstrap marketing there is an additional goal—to reach these customers by using the least amount of cash as possible.

Levinson and Godin (1994) identify the following basic principles that guide bootstrap marketing:[7]

1. ***Know the customer.*** To effectively and efficiently market to their customers, entrepreneurs should seek to understand their customers' needs and expectations. Understand the features and level of quality they want, the price they are willing to pay, and where they typically go to get information to make a purchase decisions. In other words, *learn to think like the customer.* Entrepreneurs who do not fully understand their customers should find ways to get to know them and better understand their needs. It is important for entrepreneurs to avoid attributing their own needs, expectations, and preferences to their customers, as they may be very different. For example, a young, very artistic architect was trying to build his business designing homes. In his first several designs he put the type of design and features into the homes that *he* would want—all unique looking homes with unusual floor plans that would be very expensive to build. But, his home designs would not sell because he had designed homes that were too unusual and too pricey for the average home buyer. His potential customers wanted a basic home that was affordable to build and that would be easy to resell in the future. The architect soon learned to adapt his style to meet his *customers'* expectations, rather than his own tastes and preferences. Once he made this change in his business he began to see success in selling designs.

2. ***Focus is on impact of message, not volume.*** Because of their massive advertising budgets and broad target markets, large corporations pursue an advertising strategy known as mass promotion—also known as a shotgun approach to marketing. Expensive campaigns using television and other mass media reach many people who are not, and never will be, customers. But, this may actually be the most efficient way for many larger businesses to reach their customers. However, entrepreneurs with limited cash cannot afford to waste their message on those for whom it is not intended. Their marketing strategies must be more targeted, reaching only those who are or are likely to become customers. For example, a national credit card company that wishes to reach small-business owners may spend hundreds of millions of dollars on massive direct mail and television advertising strategies reaching millions of small-business owners. The actual number of people who respond to these promotions is often less

than 1 percent of those who receive the direct mailings and even less for television ads. An entrepreneur attempting to market a service to other small-business owners could not afford to spend this type of money using strategies with such low success rates. Instead, entrepreneurs must emphasize marketing strategies and tactics that focus on those who are most likely to become customers. (We examine the most commonly used bootstrap marketing tools used to reach an entrepreneur's targeted customers in the next section of this chapter.)

3. *Focus on benefits the product/service brings to the customer.*   Bootstrap marketing should help customers understand why they should choose this product over those offered by those competing against the entrepreneurial venture. In the focused message to the targeted customers the entrepreneur should highlight special benefits offered by the product, how the product is delivered to the customer, and services that go with the product.

4. *Understand the market niche.*   In a niche strategy, the entrepreneur finds a small part of a market that is not being served or is significantly underserved. A niche strategy gives the entrepreneur a more attractive market with less competition and a more dependent set of customers. It is a common entry strategy into the market employed by new businesses, as it usually takes fewer resources because of lower marketing costs and the ability to start on a smaller scale. Success rates tend to be higher for niche businesses because they have less direct competition. Also, with less competition, niche businesses can charge higher prices, which allows for quicker positive cash flow during start-up and better margins once profitable. For example, an entrepreneur in Minneapolis recognized that all of the charter boats operating on a local lake focused on large groups of fifty or more people. His research revealed that there were many smaller groups of ten to fifteen people who wanted to book a charter boat that were not being served in this market. The entrepreneur recognized this unserved market niche and began what became a successful charter business designed to serve the smaller groups' needs.

But, there are some cautions that an entrepreneur should be aware of with a niche strategy:

- *Entering a niche requires adaptability in the business plan.*   If the entrepreneur misses the mark on exactly what customers in a niche want, it doesn't matter how safe the niche is, the customers will not automatically buy.

- *Niches change.*   Niche markets—like any market—change over time. Success in a niche requires adaptation as the market changes. Even though it is a niche, the market is not isolated and is subject to the same forces and trends that can affect any market.

- *Niches can go away.*   No market is forever. Niches are the type of market that can dry up, sometimes quite suddenly. Again, adaptation can offer some hope, but if the decline is too rapid many niche businesses will fail.

- *Niches can grow.* While significant growth in the entrepreneur's market may not sound bad, it can attract more competitors. And if it grows large enough, it can attract much larger competitors.

5. *Spend marketing dollars wisely.* At times it may be possible to achieve remarkable results while spending little or no money. Other times, as will be seen in the following discussion of bootstrap marketing techniques, it is essential to spend enough money to get the quality needed to be effective. An effectively designed and executed business plan can help avoid wasted resources.

6. *Marketing is a process, not an event.* Many entrepreneurs only concentrate on marketing their businesses during the start-up or at times when business declines and revenues slow down. The most cost effective approach to marketing is for it to be a continuous part of doing business. Consistent marketing keeps the product or service in the customers' minds. A net result of the constant awareness is that when the time comes to purchase, the likelihood that customers will think of the entrepreneur's business is stronger.

Bootstrapping using entrepreneurial marketing strategies helps to assure that the limited resources available to most entrepreneurs have the maximum impact on the targeted market. The next section examines several basic marketing tools, techniques, and tactics commonly employed by start-up entrepreneurial ventures.

WORD OF MOUTH AND VIRAL MARKETING— TURNING CUSTOMERS INTO A SALES FORCE

Andy Sernovitz and Guy Kawasaki (2006) define *word of mouth marketing* as simply "everything you can do to get people talking" about a business.[8] Word of mouth is a common marketing strategy in start-up entrepreneurial ventures. In fact, one recent poll found that 82 percent of entrepreneurs use word of mouth to grow their business while 15 percent rely almost exclusively on word of mouth.[9] However, what many aspiring entrepreneurs fail to recognize is that word of mouth rarely just happens—they fall into the myth of "if we build it, they will come." Spontaneous word of mouth is a rare event. Successful word of mouth promotion usually requires that actively finding ways to motivate customers to talk about a business in a positive way.

Kevin Jennings, founder of soundAFX, describes the benefits of word of mouth and how he makes it work for his sonic branding[10] company this way: "Word of mouth is an incredible way for marketing. The more people I meet, the more connections are formed. People know people who know people who know people. If you are good at what you do, people will refer you to others. This not only helps you, but it makes the person referring you look good and well-connected to know other talented people who can get a particular job done."

Although word of mouth promotion is often considered "free advertising," many business owners find that word of mouth is most effective when some marketing dollars are committed to help foster and encourage word of mouth.

Entrepreneurs can use several commons methods to encourage word of mouth promotion. Examples of these methods include the following:

- *Motivate customers to talk about you through excellence in customer service.*   Customer service affects customers' attitudes about a business.[11] Because there is a widespread perception of declines in customer service in the United States, an entrepreneurial venture that can create an exceptional experience through customer service can stand out and motivate customers to tell others. Entrepreneurs should understand that effective service is consistent, genuine, and enthusiastic. For example, one independent, family-owned tire retailer has been able to successfully compete against large national discounters in a large suburban market by offering exceptional service. This has been the hallmark of this business since its launching. It is common when new residents move into this suburb to get several recommendations to use this tire store from satisfied customers. In fact, the majority of the firm's new customers come from such referrals.

- *Create incentives to spread the word through a referral "thank you" program.*   New businesses can build customer loyalty and foster word of mouth by offering customers a "thank you" when they refer people to the business. Such a program can include discount coupons, a small thank you gift such as a gift card, or just a hand-written thank you note for each new customer a person sends to the entrepreneur's firm. For example, an entrepreneur who opened an independent real estate company routinely sends out a gift basket with a hand-written thank you note when past clients refer new customers. This has allowed her to compete with the larger established businesses in the market. Ask your customer to "sell" for you. Although it is not as common and not always reliable, there are businesses that early adopter customers want to see succeed so that they can keep buying from that business. This happens most often when a business fills a niche that has not been addressed in the market, thus serving a high level of pent-up demand. It is a business that clearly gets early customers excited. In this case, the entrepreneur/business owner should actively ask clients to spread the word—to let them know that the new venture needs them to help bring *in new customers in order to succeed.*

- *Create a "buzz campaign."*   It is possible to mimic word of mouth by getting friends, family, and employees to actively create a "buzz" about a business. In these instances, these individuals try to "prime the pump" of the process of word of mouth. This has become a common technique in the entertainment industry. Many fan groups are actively enlisted to get the word out about a new artist. This can also be done through a user group, who in exchange for free service, support, and education, can become a "sales force" for a new business.

  "Buzz campaigns" can be effective in building interest and pent-up demand for a business even before it opens its doors. This helps to increase the customer flow from the first day of operation. One of the keys when creating a

buzz before the business opens is timing. It should be executed soon enough to actually build a buzz and create demand prior to opening, but not so early that people lose interest or assume the business is never going to open. For example, when Bob Bernstein opened the first coffee shop in his chain of stores located in Nashville, Tennessee, he effectively used a buzz campaign.

During the renovation [of the new coffee shop], people from the neighborhood constantly came in and out of the store. They all wanted to know when the new shop would open. Eventually, Bob put a homemade canvas/burlap sign out in the front yard that said, "Bongo Java, Open Soon." The same sign hung out front (with the "Soon" cut off) for the next three years. . . . On opening day there was a line of customers out the door. Bongo Java had opened under budget and was profitable in its first month.[12]

The Internet has created a new form of word of mouth promotion, known as *viral marketing*. Whereas traditional word of mouth traveled from person to person, viral marketing uses the Internet's power to spread the word about a business exponentially through Web sites, blogs, and e-mail. Advanta, Inc., tapped into the power of viral marketing when launching its new Web site called ideablob.com, which is a Web site that conducts a monthly online contest where people can post ideas for new businesses and try to win a cash award. The winner is determined by people who visit the site and vote for their favorite idea for that month. The developers of the site used viral marketing to promote the site, relying on outlets such as YouTube, business blogs, and other media to spread the word about ideablob.com. Box 6-1 tells the story of the ideablob.com viral marketing campaign.

Finally, in addition to using customers to spread word of mouth, many entrepreneurs have also learned to harness a group that at first glance may not seem to be a logical source of business—their competitors. Many start-ups fill a niche in the market that larger competitors choose not to serve. The sales generated from serving these customers are not efficient for the larger firm to support. In many cases, these large competitors are more than happy to refer this business to a reputable smaller firm. Here are a couple of examples:

- A start-up company in Wisconsin, a state where major paper manufacturers have many larger facilities, was able to establish a small corrugated box business in the shadow of these larger companies. The start-up specialized in small-run box orders, often just a few hundred boxes per order, for small businesses in the area. The larger companies could not cost effectively meet the needs of these small businesses, as their minimum order size was typically at least tens of thousands of boxes. The large companies became one of the best sources of business for the start-up box company. They were happy to refer this business out.

- A start-up photography business was able to specialize in small shoots that required only a single photographer with simple equipment. Large photographers in the market had minimum photography package prices that were

---

BOX 6-1

The Story of the ideablob.com Viral Marketing Campaign

Viral marketing is unique. You can strategize about it and kindle it, but beyond that, you have little control over it. Despite the inherent risks, there is no better (or cheaper) method to reach millions of people, quickly.

ideablob launched at DEMO in August 2007 and instantly became the beneficiary of viral marketing.

At the show, it won the People's Choice Award. The winner of this award is selected by audience members "texting" their vote. Receiving this award launched the viral marketing campaign that has exploded.

There were three main components utilized in the viral marketing campaign. Traditional news media outlets and bloggers, social media sites like YouTube and passionate blobbers. Immediately following the success at DEMO, the media started writing articles. Within a couple of months, there were over 1,000 blog posts and over 100,000 Google entries about ideablob.

Today on YouTube, there are 70 million videos. Ideablob joined the millions and shared the video it presented at DEMO. Within one week, that video had been viewed by 1.3 million people. One million consumers were now familiar with ideablob without hiring a PR agency or deploying a sophisticated marketing campaign.

The passionate blobbers are ingenious in their ability to spread the word. As investors in the site (their ideas and mental capital), they serve as a freelance marketing team for ideablob as they spread the word about their great idea. They utilize traditional forms of marketing like flyers, emails, and phone calls. They also use more progressive techniques like blogging and videos.

On its face, the viral marketing campaign appears to be perfect. However, there is a downside. During this period, ideablob could not control the message. Bloggers were free to cast their opinions, good and bad. YouTube users were free to post comments about the video and share "related videos" without regulation. While most of the user-added content was complimentary, there was a fair amount of negative content. There was also a smattering of offensive and pornographic content.

To date, Advanta has not spent any money on traditional marketing on ideablob. Instead, it used its "marketing" money to create a hook—a monthly $10,000 prize for the best idea. This was buzz worthy and this fueled the viral marketing campaign.

So, is it worth exposing your product to millions of people fast but losing control of the message?

(Ami Kassar, Innovation Team, Advanta, Inc.)

---

well beyond the budget of many smaller customers. Their standard approach included multiple photographers using specialized equipment. Several of these larger firms referred small jobs to the start-up, finding it helped build a good reputation in the market for taking care of customers. They also got some of these small customers back as their needs grew and the small photographer was no longer able to meet the needs of these customers.

PUBLICITY

Publicity is when a news outlet writes a story about a business. Many describe it as "free" advertising, although this can be a bit of a misnomer. There is a certain amount of time that is required to get publicity about a business. And at times entrepreneurial firms find it is more effective to hire a firm, called a *public relations firm* that specializes in securing publicity for a business. However, many entrepreneurs find that they can become very effective at securing their own publicity, as described by Joe Keeley in *Start-Ups on a Shoestring* (see Box 6-2). Start-up businesses can be by their very nature newsworthy, so seeking publicity to get free coverage with media outlets is a common strategy for new ventures.

To gain publicity, the first step is to communicate to media outlets. The common device to provide information for consideration is called a *press release*. A press release is basically a pre-written article that local media can use as written or it can be a way to entice the reporters to follow-up and develop a more in-depth story. To catch the attention of journalists, entrepreneurs must clearly communicate the "hook" of the story. What is it that makes the story interesting and newsworthy? Start-up businesses are interesting, but it helps to add the "hook," offering some interesting aspect of the business, its history or the founders' background. For example, students who start businesses while in college tend to continue to be popular stories that journalists find interesting and even intriguing. Figure 6-1 displays a common template for a news release. Using a standard format is important as it communicates to reporters or editors that what you have sent them is in fact a news release. Entrepreneurs should proofread the news release very carefully before sending it out to journalists—remember that they write for a living, so the quality of the writing in the release is a crucial step in the process of encouraging journalists to consider the entrepreneur's story.

BOX 6-2   START-UPS ON A SHOESTRING

Publicity

One of those micro-marketing tactics is sending out press releases when I was a student entrepreneur but telling the story on University Letterhead. We sent it out and there was instant credibility. We wanted to be considered rather than disregarded.

When marketing and advertising and trying to get publicity, you need to know three things. Know your audience, know your angle, and take action. Know your audience: address the writers. Angle: Make it news worthy. You have to find some angle they will be interested in. 'Student Male is Running a Nanny Company.' This gets their attention. Pick up the phone and call them and send emails and newsletters.

(Joe Keeley, founder of College Nannies and Tutors, a nationally franchised company)

After writing the news release it needs to be sent to local media that might have an interest. It helps when entrepreneurs do their homework about local news outlets to learn which cover business news, and even which reporters seem to cover start-ups. It is common practice to send news releases via e-mail. The news release can be included in the body of the e-mail or as an attachment. Either way it is helpful to include a short personal message to the reporter or editor explaining why you are sending the news release, and if possible why you think it might be of interest to them and their readers. It is also good to thank them for considering the story. If the entrepreneur establishes a positive relationship with certain journalists, he or she can feel comfortable with the decision to send stories to them every few weeks or even every couple of months. However, entrepreneurs should not limit themselves to a single type of media outlet; indeed, news releases should be sent to newspapers, magazines, radio, television, and bloggers. Joe Keeley was able to get multiple stories in all types of media outlets as he started his company College Nannies and Tutors.

Entrepreneurs can follow-up with a second e-mail if their initial effort does not receive a response. More than two or three e-mails about a single news release are probably sufficient, though.

FIGURE 6-1   Template for Press Release

FOR IMMEDIATE RELEASE

CONTACT:
Contact Person
Company Name
Voice Phone Number
FAX Number
E-mail Address
Web Site

Headline *(Write a short, clear descriptive headline that lets a reporter know exactly what the story is about)*

City, State, Date—The first paragraph again tells what the story is about and presents the "hook" for the story. The style should always be factual—not written like a sales pitch. The goal is to write a short article that the newspaper can use with very little editing.

The next paragraphs should follow the style of a good news article, answering the "who," "what," "when," "where," "why," and "how" questions. Include details that assume that the reader does not know anything about the business. Sentences should be clear and short. Paragraphs should also be short. Read newspaper articles to get a sense of the style that journalists would use. Again, stick to factual writing and do not get into a sales pitch. Keep the entire news release to about 400–600 words.

The final paragraph is the "about" section of the release. It should describe the business, using the kind of language found in a clear and concise mission statement.

NEW APPROACHES TO INTERNET-BASED BOOTSTRAP MARKETING

BLOGGING

The Internet continues to create new opportunities for bootstrap marketing. Blogging is a new opportunity that has caught on with many small businesses and high growth entrepreneurial ventures. A blog, which is a shortened version of the technical term *Web log*, is an online journal that typically focuses on a specific topic. For example, the author's blog *The Entrepreneurial Mind* (http://www. drjeffcornwall.com/) offers information on small business and entrepreneurship through daily entries. People come to blogs through search engines, recommendations from friends, links from Web sites, and so forth.

A recent survey of entrepreneurs reports that 10 percent of small businesses were using or were planning to use blogs for their businesses.[13] Entrepreneurs can use blogging to establish themselves as experts within their industry. For example, Anita Campbell has been able to build her small-business media and communications company in large part through her blog *Small Business Trends*.[14] By building the readership of her blog, she has been able to become a popular small-business speaker and expert in emerging small-business trends.

A blog allows for targeted contact of customers and potential customers who are drawn to the blog by their interest in its specific content. As with a newsletter, a blog is a forum to share useful information and expertise. But unlike a newsletter, a blog creates a much more personal relationship with the visitors to the blog because of its frequency and informal style. Most bloggers find that by posting short entries at least once a week—daily is even more effective—they can build traffic at their site. Most blogs attempt to create a personal relationship with their readers. The search engine Google favors blogs in how it creates rankings in searches through that site.[15] Because of this, a blog can be a tool to drive customers to the entrepreneur's Web site and increase traffic over what he or she could hope to attract simply using only a traditional Web site.

Entrepreneurs should understand though that there are several cautions to keep in mind when attempting to use blogging as a marketing tool:

- Be consistent—most blogs take a long time to build traffic at the site. An entrepreneur needs to commit time every week to writing blog posts. It takes consistent posting over time to build awareness and traffic.

- Be cautious about what you say—writing about topics that are too controversial can actually drive away potential customers. Successful business bloggers learn to walk the delicate line between writing about interesting subject areas that keep people coming to the site and wandering into inflammatory and/or controversial topics that can drive them away forever.

- Avoid crossing the line and becoming too self-serving—blog readers will not come back to sites that are simply marketing materials for a business. People won't continue to visit a site that is simply a series of advertisements for a business. Although promotion can be part of the site through informational pages linked to from the blog site, the blog's content should never become simply promoting the business.

- Remember that the *whole world* can read what is said on a blog — this includes the entrepreneur's employees, competitors, banker and so forth. Before making any post, entrepreneurs should keep this reality in mind.

STREET TEAMS

Street teams were first used as a means of organizing fans to promote appearances of musical groups. The fans go to places where people who are likely to attend a musical event typically congregate to promote the event by passing out flyers, talking up the group to people, handing out stickers, and so forth. Other businesses have also found that street teams can be an effective promotional tool. These businesses recruit customers or hire people who fit into the target market group to engage in "on the street" promotions. For example, Howard Brauner, founder of Bald Guyz, has used street teams to promote his grooming products for bald men since launching his business.

> Knowing that his customers congregate at the NBA All-Star Game and the Super Bowl, Brauner plans to take his Bald Guyz street team to those cities during the craziness. Whether it's passing out bright blue and orange shirts that say "Bald Guys Are Sexy" or encouraging customers to send in their photos to be the Bald Guy of the Week at www.baldguyz.com, Brauner is boldly getting his brand name to consumers and his products onto the shelves of drugstores and supermarkets nationwide like Albertsons and Walgreens.[16]

WEB 2.0

Entrepreneurs are finding that some of the social Web sites that are part of Web 2.0 are proving to be effective tools for marketing their businesses. Sites such as FaceBook and MySpace allow entrepreneurs to reach a network of people with common interests. For example, Kate Singleton successfully used the bulletin feature of MySpace to spread the word about her photography business to bands and other entertainers seeking experienced photographers to take promotional photographs for them. She found that this generated most of the leads she needed to grow her new venture.

ONLINE DIRECTORIES AND CLASSIFIED LISTINGS

Online directories are quickly replacing the print version of the yellow pages. Craiglist. org is one of the most popular online directory sites.[17] Tim Anderson uses craigslist to promote his construction business:

> At Done-Rite Construction Inc., we utilize craigslist.org as one source for advertising our painting services. For Done-Rite, craigslist is a

great means of advertising for three reasons: its cost, user-friendliness, and aiming at our target market. The cost of using craigslist is what we love the most: it's free! And not only is it free, but it is very easy for our company to post ads about our painting services with pictures to show the quality of our work. After clicking on our state and region, we are connected with people who live in our area. Generally, the business that is generated from our craigslist ads are computer savvy, entrepreneurial-minded people. Many already are craigslist junkies who love to do business there and know how to find what they are looking for. Craigslist has been a great tool to help our business get off the ground.

DON'T FORGET THE BASICS—SIMPLE BOOTSTRAP MARKETING TOOLS FOR NEW VENTURES

It has been said that "necessity is the mother of invention." When it comes to marketing, the creativity of bootstrapping entrepreneurs in the face of limited resources can be quite remarkable. Countless examples of clever methods of getting information to potential customers can be found every day in the entrepreneurial economy. This section highlights some of the basic marketing tools and techniques that are most traditionally used for bootstrapping a start-up venture through marketing activities. We begin this discussion by examining what is arguably the most basic marketing tool of all—the business card.

THE BUSINESS CARD

Even in the digital age, one of the first marketing tools for almost every start-up entrepreneur is still one of the most simple—the business card. Business cards remain a standard part of business etiquette. When business people first meet it is still customary to exchange business cards. In fact, the globalization of business has made the business card an even more important marketing tool. In many Asian cultures, the exchange of business cards is a critical aspect of business etiquette and is governed by specific cultural norms of behavior.

In larger companies, new employees are automatically issued a box of standard business cards that is often waiting for them on their desks when they start their new jobs. Like many other aspects of a start-up business, entrepreneurs must create their own business cards. Because for many start-up entrepreneurs the business card may be their only form of advertising, decisions about what the card looks like, what it includes, and how it is used can be essential in connecting with their first customers. Even for an established business the business card often provides the first contact and the first impression.

Although this is a book about bootstrapping, it is important to keep in mind the definition of bootstrapping from Chapter 1 when developing business cards. Remember, bootstrapping is not just finding the cheapest way to do something.

It is always about creating the desired impact within the constraints of limited resources. Thus, entrepreneurs need to think about how the design, look, and feel of the business card represent their venture. The business card communicates a great deal about the entrepreneur and his or her business. It is an important element in creating the first impression that any potential customer or client will take away from an initial meeting. For example, if the card looks cheap and hand-made, it can communicate that the entrepreneur's business is not professional and may not even be a stable and reliable firm with which to do business. Figure 6-2 is an example of a business card designed by an entrepreneur for his music publishing business.

The following is a list of considerations entrepreneurs should consider when developing a business card for their start-up venture:

- ***Basic design decisions.***   Even though a business card is fairly small and simple, there are a number of basic design issues to consider:
  - White space can be used to help draw people's eyes to critical information
  - The feel of the card can be enhanced by using embossing or textured paper

FIGURE 6-2   Sample Business Card for a Start-Up Company

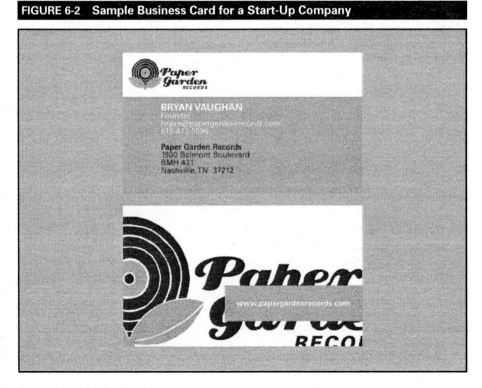

Source: Paper Garden Records

- Although some businesses are experimenting with different sizes or even nonstandard shapes of cards, most experts recommend using a standard size and shape so people recognize that it is actually a business card—this increases the odds they will retain the card for future reference
- Although horizontal printing (see Figure 6-2) is standard, many cards are now being printed vertically to grab the customer's attention
- A photograph of the entrepreneur can help jog a customer's memory as to who gave the card

- ***Include all critical data, but only if it is useful.*** Business cards should include all important contact information. If clients will only contact a venture by phone, it may not be necessary to include such things as a mailing address. And if most business will be conducted by cell phone, or if a client needs to have ready access to the entrepreneur, make sure to include a cell phone number. If an entrepreneur has a Web site that provides important information for a potential customer, the Web address should be made prominent on the business card. Businesses that have their customers visiting the place of business should include the physical address on the card. A business card is part of the tools used to communicate to the customer; because of this, entrepreneurs should make certain that the critical contact information that needs to be accessible to any customer is included. The example business card in Figure 6-2 includes a mailing address, e-mail address, cell phone number and Web site address for the entrepreneur, since all of these may be used at one time or another by customers of this new record label.

- ***Paper.*** Top-quality paper is important. A card printed off of a home computer on perforated paper tends to make the business appear as if it is not permanent nor even a "real" business. A professional printer using the best paper that the entrepreneur can afford should do the printing. This is another example of when it is important to spend money, but spend it wisely. According to John Williams, author and advertising executive, "Touch is an important sense and plays a role in memory recall. How you appeal to this sense depends on your company's image. For example, B2B companies wanting to convey reliability should use a substantial, mid-weight stock."[18]

- ***Color.*** Colored ink can make a card stand out. Most experts suggest using at least two colors of ink. Standard colors are much less expensive than custom blended colors, so it may be advisable to try to stick to standard colors offered by the printer. Author Rhonda Abrams has this additional advice on the use of color on business cards: "Be careful with color to make certain your information remains clearly readable. Light colored ink on dark paper is very difficult to read, as is pale colored ink, even on white paper. Choose colors that are appropriate to your line of business and to you. A lawyer probably wouldn't want to have any pink to their card—a florist or child-care center might."[19] The example in Figure 6-2 uses three colors of ink—black, green and white.

- *Include description or slogan.*   Most cards have room to include a brief description of the business or a slogan. Because cards may be one of the only forms of advertising for a new business, it is recommended that such information be included on the card. While a full mission statement will probably include too many words for a business card, a short phrase that describes what the business offers or how it wants to be remembered in terms of its quality or commitment to customer satisfaction can easily fit on a card and help reinforce an important message to customers.

- *Remember, it has two sides.*   If getting more content onto the business card is important, it is possible to include additional information on the back side. However, printing on the back will usually increase the card's cost. Information that businesses place on the back of cards often includes noncontact related information such as pricing, a map with directions, or a photo of the product. Slogans, descriptions of the business, and logos also can be included on the back (Figure 6-2 has an example). However, Rhonda Abrams offers the following caution about printing on the back of a card: "I used to have beautiful cards with my logo printed against a complete black background on the reverse side. But people were frustrated that they couldn't write notes on the back, such as where they met me. That doesn't mean the back side of your card has to remain blank. Use it to print more information about your business or even to give a discount. Just remember, once someone has put your card in a file or a drawer, they'll probably never see the reverse side again."[20]

Because for many entrepreneurs the business card is an important marketing tool it is important to have a plan on how to use the card and more specifically how to get it into the hands of potential customers. Ivan Misner in his book *It's in the Cards!* offers the following tactics for using a business card most effectively:[21]

- *Make your cards accessible in every situation.*   Keep a supply of cards in multiple places to assure one is always available when the need arises. Put a supply in your brief case, in your car, in your wallet, in your purse, and in the pockets of your business suit coats. And if business partners, family members, or loyal customers regularly give out your cards, make sure they always have a steady supply.

- *Seek situations to exchange business cards.*   Face-to-face interactions with customers offer an opportunity to give out not only business cards, but other promotional materials. Also, networking events hosted by the Chamber of Commerce or other business groups offer opportunities to meet people and pass out business cards. Trade shows and professional conferences are good places to pass out cards to potential customers and customer referral sources.

- *Noncompeting and complementary businesses.*   Many businesses will be happy to keep a supply of your business cards and may even allow you to set up a small business card holder in their business. For example, a paint store is happy to keep a supply of business cards for professional house painters. The paint store manager will benefit from the painter buying paint from the store and making the painting process easier for the customer. Other examples include landscapers putting cards in a retail plant nursery and Web designers and computer consultants leaving cards at a retail computer store.

- *Contacts at a distance.*   Whenever communicating with a customer, include a business card (or even several cards). This can include when mailing a brochure, shipping products, general correspondence, and sending a thank you note.

The electronic business card, often referred to as an e-card, has gained in usage over the past several years. The e-card can be used to provide contact information that can be contained in people's e-mail address books, hand-held planners, and increasingly in cell phones. But even in the digital age, the e-card is still considered a supplement to the standard printed business card. The exchange of the business card will likely remain a standard part of business protocol and etiquette, particularly in global business relationships, for years to come.

WEB SITES

Twenty years ago, in addition to getting business cards printed, most new business owners would place a listing in the yellow pages of the phone book. The yellow pages were the most common place for people to find information about start-up ventures as well as small businesses. In fact for many small businesses, the yellow pages were the main form of advertising. Today, Web sites on the Internet have taken the place of the yellow pages for many start-up businesses. Just as twenty years ago most start-ups got a yellow pages listing, today most start-ups launch a Web site as a way for people to find information about their business.

When planning and developing a Web site, entrepreneurs must understand its usefulness for potential and existing customers. Just as is the case with any promotional tool, it is important for entrepreneurs to think like their customers when making decisions about the Web site. The design should be one that appeals to customers. For example, Charles Hagood is co-founder of an engineering consulting firm. Hagood's original business involved consulting with manufacturing companies. Most of the customers from the manufacturing companies were engineers. They preferred a great deal of text and detail, as that is what they are used to in their work. Hagood later launched a new business providing process consulting to healthcare companies. Hagood discovered that the intended customers of each line of business had a very different expectations and preferences when going to a Web site for information. The potential customers from healthcare facilities were used to Web sites from hospitals and insurance companies that tended to have a lot less text and more of a focus on visual presentations (usually photographs of health care professionals). Therefore, Hagood had to develop a distinctive Web site with a very different style and with a "look" that was consistent with customer expectations from the healthcare customer base.

Web sites generally serve three basic purposes: (1) promotion, (2) communication, and (3) order processing. Some Web sites do only one or two of these functions, while some do all three. The more functions a Web site has, the more expensive it is to develop and maintain. While many entrepreneurs can create their own site that promotes their business and/or offers basic communication, developing an effective Web site to conduct e-commerce generally requires hiring a web developer. An e-commerce Web site can easily cost thousands or even tens of thousands of dollars to develop. Therefore, when e-commerce is a critical component of a business model for a start-up it is essential to account for these costs in the start-up budget. Also, many e-commerce sites require frequent updates to keep product listings and other time sensitive or important information up to date. Web site updates and maintenance should also be carefully and realistically planned for and budgeted for an e-commerce site.

One of the main differences between the yellow pages of the twentieth century and a Web site in the twenty-first century is that the listings in a yellow page directory were all in one single location (the phone book) organized by a simple scheme of business categories. A Web site is housed on the Internet with millions of other Web sites with billions of pages. Search engines can help customers find some Web sites, but they do not offer much help to a new business since they list sites based on existing traffic to the Web sites. Therefore, a start-up entrepreneur planning to use a Web site should develop a plan to drive people to the site. A simple way to get people to the site is to include the Web address on all other forms of promotion, such as business cards, brochures, signs, and any form of advertising (e.g., radio, television, newspapers, magazines, etc.). Another means to drive people to a Web site is to use search engine optimization techniques to drive the Web site up higher in common search engines, such as Google and Yahoo. The ultimate goal is to get a site to be on the first page of Google when certain key words or search terms are entered.

One means of driving more people to a Web site is called *organic placement*. Web sites that get a lot of traffic can move up the rankings of the key search engines. For example, as of this writing the author's blog site, *The Entrepreneurial Mind*, comes up in the top five placements in Google when the word *entrepreneurial* is typed into the search engine. It generally comes in at the very top when *Jeff Cornwall* is typed in the search engine. I did not pay to have this placement. It happened because I have been blogging about entrepreneurship for several years and have built up a substantial amount of traffic and a large number of links to my blog. The positive aspect of organic placement is that it is free. The negative aspects are that it takes time to develop (years in the case of my blog) and that it does not always work on the best and most commonly used phrases. For example, if the words *entrepreneur* or *entrepreneurship* are typed into Google, which probably are what would be the most common words that people would use, my blog is nowhere to be seen among the top placements. The same thing happens when you type in *Cornwall* rather than *Jeff Cornwall*.

The alternative to organic placement is to pay for placement, which can become a very expensive approach. There are two basic methods to pay for placement in search engines: pay per click and becoming a sponsored site. It is best for entrepreneurs to work with experts in search engine optimization, making sure to interview more than one. Entrepreneurs should check experts' references carefully, making sure to talk to clients who have a somewhat similar business with a similar budget. And, entrepreneurs need to be clear with the search engine optimization firm about their expectations and their budget. Unless a business has an e-commerce business model, it may not be necessary to pay for search engine placement for most start-up businesses.

BROCHURES

Brochures can be an inexpensive means of providing a visual presentation of the business. For a new business it provides a more comprehensive format to educate potential customers about the business and its products and services. Developing an effective brochure requires understanding the expectations of potential customers. It is easy to both underspend and overspend on design and production. As an example of overspending, a health care entrepreneur spent thousands of dollars to design and produce a full-color, glossy brochure only to find that the customers thought that the brochure communicated all style and no substance regarding the entrepreneur's new clinic. The customers, in this case referring physicians, would have been much more attracted to a simpler brochure that highlighted the factual details of the clinic's programs. On the other hand, an entrepreneur with a new commercial cleaning business provides an example of underspending. This entrepreneur made a hand-written brochure that she copied herself at a neighborhood copy store. The other cleaners she was competing against were distributing professionally printed brochures. In this example, the entrepreneur's brochure was not effective because hers was hand-made and did not meet the basic standards set by her competitors.

Levinson and Godin (1994) identify two important marketing advantages that a properly designed brochure can provide.[22] First, having a brochure can create an immediate increase in credibility for a new entrepreneur. The brochure gives the impression that the entrepreneur has created a legitimate business that has a past and a future. Second, a brochure can decrease the immediate pressure on customers to make a decision. It gives the customer information that can be evaluated when she is ready to consider it, while still capturing the basic sales pitch.

Bootstrapping entrepreneurs often complete much of the developmental work on brochures themselves. However, these brochures will be seen alongside those from established businesses in their market which may have used professional advertising and design firms to develop their materials. The bootstrapping entrepreneur should incorporate several basic design features when creating a brochure. By working on this basic information and even developing some of the design of the brochure before meeting with a graphic designer or printer, the entrepreneur can realize significant savings on the design costs while still resulting in a professional brochure that will compete with brochures produced for larger and more established companies:

1. Be sure to tailor the brochure to the customers' expectations. Collect as many competitors' brochures as possible for comparison, and if possible, talk with a few customers to get their reaction to some of the more common designs.
2. Include a clear headline on the brochure. This should be more than the company name. It should clarify what business the company is in.
3. Brochures should be visually appealing. If not, customers are less likely to read them. This requires considering visual features such as graphics, white space, logos, and photographs.
4. The brochure should tell the venture's story and make a good sales pitch.
5. If possible, it may be helpful to include a list of customers and testimonials.
6. As is the case with a business card, a brochure should include useful contact information including such things as a map if the customer will be coming to the place of business.
7. Order forms or information request forms can help increase the likelihood of action by the customer.

The current digital age has created new media for brochures that takes the information off the printed page and moves it to various digital formats. DVD brochures can create a much stronger visual presentation of a product or service. For example, a newly opened private boarding school that specialized in teaching troubled children needed to reassure parents of potential students that the school was a safe and nurturing environment. Because students came to this school from across the United States, the owner wanted to be able to communicate this message visually to parents who may not be able to visit the school before they enroll their children. A DVD brochure was developed that proved to be very effective. It was sent only to parents who had inquired about the school to help keep costs in line. Another example is when Select Comfort, a manufacturer of air filled mattresses, first entered its chosen market. The DVD brochure Select Comfort developed had two goals. The first was to visually show that the firm's product was a real mattress and not an air mattress used by campers under their sleeping bags. The second was to demonstrate the ease of setting up the mattress, as this had been an issue that previously caused resistance to buying the product. Again, the DVD brochure was sent to interested potential customers to keep costs down. This video brochure also proved to be effective.

BANNERS, SIGNS, AND TRADE SHOW DISPLAYS

Banners are commonly used to draw attention to a new business to announce that it is "now open." Banners are typically used in businesses, such as retail, where the customer comes directly to the place of business. Entrepreneurs can use a variety of banners and signs to bring attention to their businesses. Banners and signs can help draw attention to the business location, promote special offers, highlight new products, and so forth. They also help to clearly identify location of the business for new customers.

Signs can be used by service companies to identify places where they are working on a job or jobs they have recently finished. Examples might include lawn signs used by home repair companies or magnetic signs on trucks and equipment of a landscaping business that are parked outside a job site. The signs draw attention to the type and quality of the work being performed. These signs can help bring awareness to new businesses that have not yet gained market awareness.

When designing banners and signs it is important to carefully proofread all text, as it is the entrepreneur's responsibility to do so. Although banners and signs are relatively inexpensive, it is wise to use materials that will last with normal use and be visually attractive to customers.

Trade shows are a good opportunity for business-to-business marketing. For a new venture it can be an effective way to announce its entry into the market and to connect with a large group of potential customers in a single event. Trade shows typically feature tabletop or floor displays that are used to attract the attention of potential customers at the trade show. Because the entrepreneur will be competing with other businesses for the attention of the attendees, it is important to have a display that is at least comparable in appearance. Before purchasing a display, the entrepreneur should determine whether or not it will get enough use to justify the cost—it should not be used as a one-time marketing tool. Entrepreneurs can save part of the development cost of the display by creating some of the visual items themselves. Lighting is important for the display, as trade shows are often held in large poorly lit facilities, such as convention centers.

NEWSLETTERS

A newsletter that is sent to customers is another basic marketing tool. Newsletters are an effective tool for a new business to establish a relationship with its customers. Most newsletters are sent out on a routine basis, usually quarterly. There are various formats for newsletters, but most range from one to eight pages in length. To increase the likelihood that the newsletter is read by the customer, it should be interesting, informative, and educational. The content can be a mix of articles related to the entrepreneur's industry and some that highlight the company itself. When possible, it also can be a good idea to highlight customers in the newsletter. If the company itself produces the newsletter, it is important to proofread carefully and to keep the content tightly written. A top quality design will increase readership, and the design should be kept consistent over time. The focus and type of content should also be kept consistent over time. In some industries there are template newsletters with industry articles already written. The company name is inserted at the top, and there is room for the company to write an article or two of its own. Finally, once a business starts a newsletter, there should be a commitment to continue it over time. Customers can become disaffected when a newsletter that they have grown to anticipate stops arriving in the mail.

Electronic newsletters are quickly replacing print newsletters for many businesses; for a new venture, electronic newsletters can provide widespread market awareness. An advantage of the electronic newsletter, particularly for a start-up venture on a limited budget, is that it can be much less expensive to distribute than a traditional paper newsletter. Although there is the cost associated with setting up the template, which is often outsourced to a e-mailing company, this tends to be much less expensive than the cost of printing and mailing a paper newsletter.

Conclusion and Summary

This chapter examined the bootstrap marketing techniques common to start-up businesses. Tools and techniques presented in this chapter include blogs, word of mouth (also known as viral marketing), and publicity. But, as we have discussed, bootstrap marketing also includes some of the most simple marketing tools—the business card, brochures, signs, and Web sites. Chapter 7 continues this examination of bootstrap marketing, discussing additional tools and techniques that entrepreneurs use in growing ventures.

Discussion Questions

1. Describe the philosophy of bootstrap marketing.
2. Design a business card for a start-up venture. Describe the design choices made in creating the layout for the business card.
3. Design a brochure for an entrepreneurial venture. Describe the design choices made in creating the layout for the brochure.
4. What are the decisions that lead to the development of a successful Web site for a start-up business?
5. How can an entrepreneur effectively use word of mouth to market a new venture?
6. Develop a press release for a new business. Explain the steps you would take to disseminate this press release to gain media publicity for the business.
7. List and discuss the ways in which the Internet has expanded the power of bootstrap marketing.

Endnotes

1. Flamholtz, E., and Randle, Y. (2007). *Growing Pains.* 4th edition. San Francisco: Jossey-Bass.
2. Schindehutte, M., Morris, M., and Pitt, L. (2009). *Rethinking Marketing.* Upper Saddle River, NJ: Pearson Education, p. 29.
3. Vaill, P. (1996). *Learning as a Way of Being: Strategies for Survival in a World of Permanent White Water.* San Francisco: Jossey-Bass.
4. Levinson, J., and Lautenslager, A. (March 2005), *Entrepreneur.com,* http://findarticles.com/p/articles/mi_m0DTI/is_3_33/ai_n11836471, retrieved March 27, 2008.
5. Jantsch, J. (2007). *Duct Tape Marketing: The World's Most Practical Small Business Marketing Guide.* Nashville, TX: Thomas Nelson.

6. Schindehutte, M., Morris, M., and Pitt, L. (2009). *Rethinking Marketing.* Upper Saddle River, NJ: Pearson Education, p. 150.

7. Levinson, J., and Godin, S. (1994). *The Guerrilla Marketing Handbook.* Boston: Houghton-Mifflin.

8. Sernovitz, A., and Kawasaki, G. (2006). *Word of Mouth Marketing: How Smart Companies Get People Talking.* Chicago: Kaplan Publishing.

9. http://www.nfib.com/object/sbPolls.

10. Sonic branding is the use of sound, typically music, to enhance and strengthen brand identity or market an organization, product, or service. It often involves creating short songs, commonly referred to as audio logos or sonic signatures that become part of the brand of a product. For example, the short song that plays when Microsoft Windows opens on a computer is an audio logo and is apart of their overall sonic brand. When people hear that music, they associate it with Windows.

11. Bolton, R., and Drew, J. (1991). A Longitudinal Analysis of the Impact of Service Changes on Customer Attitudes. *Journal of Marketing,* 55(1), 1–9.

12. Cornwall, J. (2006) "Bongo Bob." United States Association for Small Business and Entrepreneurship, *Proceedings.*

13. http://www.nfib.com/object/sbPolls.

14. http://www.smallbiztrends.com/.

15. http://www.inc.com/magazine/20080201/more-than-idle-chatter.html, retrieved on April 4, 2008.

16. Torres, N. (2007). *Audacious Advertising,* http://www.entrepreneur.com/advertising/article173464.html, retrieved April 4, 2008.

17. http://www.craigslist.org/about/sites.html.

18. Williams, J. (2007). *Entrepreneur.com.* http://www.entrepreneur.com/marketing/branding/imageandbrandingcolumnistjohnwilliams/article185886.html, retrieved on March 28, 2008.

19. Abrams, R. (2003). Inc.com. http://www.inc.com/articles/2001/10/23657.html, retrieved on March 28, 2008.

20. Abrams, R. (2003). Inc.com. http://www.inc.com/articles/2001/10/23657.html, retrieved on March 28, 2008.

21. Misner, I. (2003). *It's in the Cards!* San Dimas, CA: Paradigm Publishing.

22. Levinson, J., and Godin, S. (1994). *The Guerrilla Marketing Handbook.* Boston: Houghton-Mifflin.

CHAPTER 7

BOOTSTRAP MARKETING: THE GROWING VENTURE

When we did our first trade show, we borrowed a booth from our next-door neighbors. Every business spends thousands of dollars on their booths, but we just went to Costco and bought bottles of water and put our label on it. We had shirts made and bought them at Target and had them embroidered with our logo. We did it inexpensively. You don't have to spend a lot of money to act like you are a big company. Everything I did was always to save money. I always made sure I knew what the result of every penny was. (Debbie Gordon, Founder of Snappy Auctions).

Overview

The Marketing Plan in Growing Ventures

Dancing with the Customer—The Role of Bootstrapping in Product Positioning

Bootstrapping Techniques to Communicate with Communities of Customers

Bootstrapping Distribution Through the Internet

Conclusion and Summary

LEARNING OBJECTIVES

✓ Understand the changing nature and role of marketing in a growing venture
✓ Explain product positioning and how it relates to bootstrapping in a growing company

✓ Examine the various bootstrap promotional strategies for a growing business
✓ Explore how the Internet has added a new channel of distribution for many businesses and how bootstrapping techniques can apply to this form of distribution

OVERVIEW

As was made clear at the beginning of this book, bootstrap marketing is not just for start-ups and small businesses. Marketing fuels growth—and this growth can create cash flow challenges that can put even seemingly successful businesses in financially difficult positions. Bootstrapping should continue to be a part of creating the marketing mix even in a growing venture. Product positioning, promotion, and distribution should all be guided by a bootstrapping philosophy. This chapter will examine these three aspects of bootstrap marketing in a growing venture.

THE MARKETING PLAN IN GROWING VENTURES

The marketing plan provides a blueprint of how entrepreneurs intend to engage the market and their customers. But the market that most entrepreneurs now are engaging is going through a fundamental transformation. The American economy today has been described as being driven by an entrepreneurial imperative.[1] The United States has seen a dramatic shift to an economy that is being shaped by entrepreneurial ventures and the opening of truly global markets. The competitive marketplace is now being driven by entrepreneurial energy and dynamic change. Over 50 percent of the nonfarm gross domestic product (GDP) is being generated by entrepreneurs.[2] Because of these fundamental changes in our economy, the orientation businesses take in their marketing strategies has also undergone a transformation.

In their book *Rethinking Marketing* from this Entrepreneurship Series Schindehutte, Morris, and Pitt (2009) explain how these changes are reflected in the traditional marketing mix that drives marketing strategy. "It therefore appears quite likely that there will be dwindling opportunities to sustain competitive advantage by attempts to simply interpret and respond to existing customer wants."[3] In other words, marketing strategy has had to shift from a reactive customer orientation to a more proactive orientation of shaping the market by true interaction with the customer. The product is not presented to the market, but it actually becomes a *co-created* solution between the business and its customers. They argue that promotion, the traditional approach to broadcasting information to the market, now becomes active *communication* with communities of like-minded people. For example, the Bongo Java coffee houses in Nashville each has a unique atmosphere and a unique menu. Since they attract people from different parts of the city, each store manager works to find the unique "product" that each market niche is looking for from the various locations in town. The product includes the look and feel of the restaurant, the food offerings on the menu, and even the blends of coffee offered. Pricing must become more *customizable*, offering personalized value. And distribution (or "place") now must address the growing demand for choice and convenience. Due to this shift from the traditional four Ps of marketing to four Cs, the marketing plan is no longer just a part of the business plan, it has become the heart of the business plan as it drives the evolution of a company's business model within this dynamic environment. The dynamic nature of the economy and the resulting shift in how entrepreneurs must react to these changes in their marketing strategies only heightens the need to continue to focus on a bootstrapping approach to marketing as a business grows.

In addition, the very nature of a growing venture adds to the need to continue to bootstrap. Arguably, growth is the most challenging time to effectively manage the cash flow in an entrepreneurial venture. Commercial bankers who work with entrepreneurs can become quite concerned when their clients hit periods of growth. They know from working with countless entrepreneurs that the success that spurs growth can often lead to the undoing of a business in which the entrepreneur is not keenly aware of the importance of careful cash flow management. As a result, bankers often restrict access to new financing for rapidly growing ventures. Escalating accounts receivable, growing inventories, and needing to add new employees and other critical resources to the business to support anticipated growth all strain cash flow. Simply put, many growing entrepreneurial ventures, particularly those in periods of high growth, fail due to their inability to effectively transition their businesses and effectively manage cash flow.[4] In addition to the short-term financial well-being of the business, improved cash flow can help improve the value of a business. Business valuation is tied to expected future cash flows. Since bootstrapping improves cash flow, continuation of bootstrapping during growth can increase valuation for the entrepreneur when he or she eventually exits the venture. Table 7-1 summarizes the reasons for bootstrap marketing in a growing venture that arise from the changing nature of marketing strategy and from the needs that result from growth in an entrepreneurial venture.

TABLE 7-1 Reasons for Bootstrap Marketing in a Growing Venture	
Due to Changes to New Marketing	*Due to the Demands of Growth*
• *Cocreated solutions*—leads to a need to be nimble in a dynamic market • *Communication with communities of customers*—more competition from growing number of new entrepreneurs increases need to be relevant and stand out • *Customizable prices*—results from growing demand for personalized value • *Choice and convenience*—the Internet has truly changed the nature of distribution and definition of market niches	• Limits on funding from banks • A desire to delay external equity funding for the venture or to keep 100 percent of the ownership in the entrepreneur's own hands • To continue to increase income and wealth from the venture for the entrepreneur by improving cash flow • The sustain the values of prudence and stewardship

Business planning remains critical in a growing entrepreneurial venture. From the previous discussion we can conclude that businesses must approach business planning as a continuous process rather than a periodic event. With the marketing plan now at the heart of the business plan, the need to gather real-time information that helps the entrepreneur continuously shape what is offered to the customer, how it is communicated to the customer, and how it creates value and is conveniently delivered to the customer is essential to sustain business growth. Traditional forms of market research that rely on periodic, large-scale assessment to gather generic and static information are no longer are feasible nor are they really effective. Growing ventures and even large, established businesses now utilize bootstrap market research techniques that were once only seen in start-up ventures. Bootstrap market research techniques include:

- *Wind-shield market research.* The entrepreneur continuously gathers information about customers and competitors by experiencing the marketplace first-hand. Secondary research and periodic traditional market surveys often result in data that is too dated in a dynamic market. The entrepreneur needs first-hand information that can be gathered by experiencing the marketplace that includes observation of customers and competitors in action.

- *Everyone is a market researcher in the company.* Critical real-time data about customers needs to be gathered by everyone who works in the business. Employees interact with customers, suppliers, and competitors. Employees also experience the broader market environment of the business and can offer information on more fundamental trends in the regulatory arena, technology, the economy, society and culture, and so forth, which can all have a significant impact on the business model. Everyone who works in the business has access to critical information that can help shape the dynamic process of business and market planning.

- *Create a "video" of the market, not a "picture."* Traditional business and market planning created a snapshot of the market at a point in time. Due to the dynamic nature of the market, the broader environment, and the constantly evolving nature of the relationship with the customer, planning should create more of an ever-changing "video" of the market, rather than the static "picture" that has been the result of traditional planning and market strategy.

Bootstrapping must therefore be a part of every aspect of the business planning process, including how market data is gathered, how this gets translated into a marketing plan, how the operational aspects of the business are carried out, and how the financial resources of the business are managed. Figure 7-1 displays a summary of the role of bootstrapping throughout the business planning process. The operating aspects of bootstrapping in a growing venture remain the same as those discussed in Chapters 2–5. Overhead, capital expenses, staffing, and processes all must continue to be bootstrapped to preserve the scarce resources

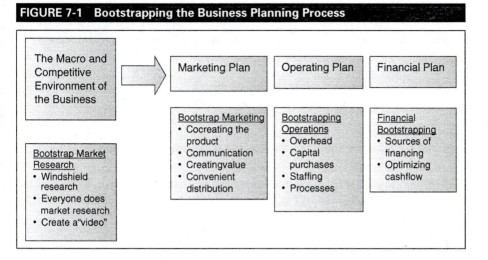

FIGURE 7-1 Bootstrapping the Business Planning Process

of the venture and to optimize the income and wealth the entrepreneur can expect from the business. Chapter 8 will examine the bootstrap management of the financial resources in a business in more detail. Chapter 9 will present how bootstrapping can be sustained in growing ventures through organizational culture. The remainder of this chapter will examine how entrepreneurial ventures put bootstrap marketing into action as they grow.

DANCING WITH THE CUSTOMER—THE ROLE OF BOOTSTRAPPING IN PRODUCT POSITIONING

The entrepreneur can no longer simply define the product during the business planning process that takes place before the launch of a venture and then work to establish a foothold in the market once the business is started. Instead, the entrepreneur must continue to "dance with the customer" to co-create over time the nature of the product and its attributes in ways that stay relevant and desirably by the customer throughout the life of the entrepreneurial venture. The dynamic nature of creating and re-creating the product requires a bootstrapping mentality. The entrepreneur must be creative, agile, and responsive to the desires of the customer within the realities of limited resources. The entrepreneur must rely on bootstrapping to guide the process of co-creating the product to assure that responses to the evolving needs of the customer are nimble and timely, and that they stay within the cash constraints that every growing venture faces.

The product sold by a business is more than simply the physical characteristics of the product. It also includes how the product is perceived by the customer in terms of a variety of features and intrinsic characteristics. Part of the marketing efforts of any business is to position their products or services in the minds of the customers based on the key criteria the target customers use to make a decision to purchase. This is known as *product positioning*. Ries and Trout (2001) describe product positioning as not what you necessarily do to the product, but rather how you place the product in the mind of the customer.[5] It is how a business differentiates their product or service from those of their competitors. Since the marketing budget of any entrepreneurial venture is limited, the bootstrapper knows that the goal is to maximize the impact of marketing efforts within the constraints of the funding available to market the business. There are three basic categories of characteristics that can be drawn upon to position a product: product variables, service variables, and personnel variables.

Product variables can include its features, performance, durability, reliability, reparability, style, and design. Product variables are generally what are used to assess its *quality*. When pricing is factored in with quality, the customer is then able to determine the value of the product as it meets their specific needs. If the quality of the product is a key criteria customers use when making a product choice, the bootstrap marketer will know to focus resources on positioning the product in the minds of the customers as being of high quality.

Service variables describe the context of how the product is offered to the customer. For example, Bob Bernstein, founder of the coffee shop chain Bongo Java, tells his employees that they do not sell coffee—they sell atmosphere and community. How the customer is treated by the staff and the environment the staff create in each uniquely designed coffee shop is what they sell to their customers.

Personnel variables include factors such as the competence and skill level of employees and the behaviors they exhibit when interacting and engaging with the customer. Personnel variables also are shaped by the ethics and values that define how employees treat customers as stakeholders of the business. This can include the employees' responsiveness to customer concerns and the integrity they bring to their work. It is important to note that product positioning is not what is communicated about these variables—that is part of promotion, which can reinforce that the product is of high quality. Instead, product positioning is accomplished by creating products and services that consistently meet these expectations. Positioning will often draw upon several of these variables to clearly position the product along key criteria critical to the target customers. For example, best quality, lowest price, best value, or most reliable are common positioning statements. Table 7-2 summarizes some of the common approaches used to position a product and the implications that should be considered for bootstrapping the entrepreneurial venture.

An example of the power of product positioning in a high growth venture is August Enterprises, which makes and installs interior and exterior signs for high-end commercial projects including hospitals and high-rise office buildings. The company founder, Tony Hatchel, has built this successful venture by positioning his product as being very high quality at a market competitive price. He is best known for the reliability of his installation. No job is considered complete until it

TABLE 7-2 Bootstrapping Implications for Product Positioning	
Positioning Variables	*Bootstrapping Implications*
Product: • Full line of product choices • Tremendous depth within product lines • Wide choice of features	A wide variety of product offerings through the breadth of the product line or depth of offering within each line can result in higher inventory costs. The same can be true of optional features. Bootstrapping favors narrower offerings to keep inventory carrying costs to the optimal level, so this should be carefully balanced against the preference expressed by customers.
Service: • Installation • Delivery • Customer support • Hours of operation • Customization • Customer interaction with staff	Added services can increase staffing costs if not properly planned. The use of outsourcing is one bootstrapping strategy that can help add service while balancing the additional costs of added services. "Employee stretching" may also become a bootstrapping tool for added service.
Personnel: • Courtesy • Knowledge and expertise • Open communication with customer	Many personnel variables can be implemented with little additional cost, making them a desirable approach for the bootstrapper. Recruiting criteria should include these factors to assure that they are met within the constraints of available staffing positions.

meets the exact specification of the job. Even though the business sells millions of dollars in signs across the country, Tony has been known to personally fly to a job site to assure that the sign and its installation meets all of the expectations of the client. He will also commit his time and the time of his staff to assure that a job meets the exacting quality expectations of each client. Over time, this approach to his product has positioned his business in the minds of commercial developers as having the best quality in the market at competitive market prices. Tony considers his approach to be one of bootstrapping, because rather than spend large sums on expensive promotional materials and traditional sales activities, he has always taken great care to carefully target the use of resources toward product positioning. As a true bootstrapper, this has helped him to meet his aggressive goals for growth within the limited budget he has available for marketing the business.

BOOTSTRAPPING TECHNIQUES TO COMMUNICATE WITH COMMUNITIES OF CUSTOMERS

Chapter 6 provided many tools and techniques that bootstrapping entrepreneurs use to get the word out about their new business, and do so within what is often a very limited budget. But since bootstrapping is not limited to start-ups and small businesses, there are many promotional strategies and tactics used by growing businesses that also adhere to the bootstrapping philosophy. Promotion is the way a business communicates to the customer all of the other parts of marketing—the product and its attributes, the price, and how they can get the product (distribution).

As stated earlier in this chapter, the new reality of business is that the entrepreneur must view promotion as communicating with a community of customers. The marketing techniques discussed in this section are tied to several of the basic principles of bootstrap marketing outlined throughout this book. They all have as their fundamental goal the efficient use of scarce marketing dollars to reach the desired community of customers. In business-to-consumer (B2C) marketing the customer group can be defined by demographic, economic, and/or geographic variables. Likewise, target markets for business-to-business (B2B) marketing can be defined by business size and/or industry segment. The bootstrapper attempts to clearly define a market niche, be it a consumer niche (B2C marketing) or a niche that defines a grouping of businesses (B2B marketing).

Snappy Auction is an example of an entrepreneurial venture that identified both types of niches to target. Originally Snappy Auction was established to facilitate the process of online auctions using eBay as its basic framework. The consumer niche was affluent people who had more expensive and valuable personal items that they wanted to sell online. While getting to know these customers, company founder Debbie Gordon found that they either did not know how to use services like eBay or just did not want to deal with the hassle of conducting their own online auction. They were willing to pay a significant fee to have the auction conducted for them. Snappy Auction sold franchise retail operations around the country that facilitated customers dropping off the items they wanted to sell. Later, Snappy Auctions also used their expertise and systems in facilitating online auctions to satisfy the needs of a business niche market. Snappy Auctions sold their system and expertise of facilitating online auctions to large corporations wanting to discard of dated capital. For example, they helped large urban hospitals to sell medical equipment that was functional but no longer state-of-the-art to rural hospitals. They also helped large corporations sell slightly used office furnishings via the Internet to small businesses. In both cases Snappy Auctions targeted a specific market niche that shared common needs. By targeting specific market niches, the entrepreneur bootstraps by focusing resources on communicating with the community of customers within that niche. It is the both an efficient and effective approach to marketing—the essence of bootstrapping. The remainder of this section will explore the techniques of marketing a growing venture that are consistent with a bootstrapping philosophy.

TARGET MARKETING

The use of promotional tools that go directly to known customers or those who have a high likelihood of becoming customers is called *target marketing*. Target marketing has a goal of a high impact on the market niche, and focuses on the specific benefits the customer will receive. Target marketing can send this message directly to customers where they live or work, through a variety of media. Quite often, this can be done through lists that send a message via direct mail, e-mail, faxes, or phone calls.

Mailing lists provide a means for contacting targeted potential customers using a variety of techniques using the traditional U.S. Postal Service or e-mails. There are many sources that sell lists that can be tailored to a specific target market. To keep the costs as low as possible, the requested list should be highly focused so it contains only likely customers. List providers can achieve this by constraining to certain customer types, zip codes, demographics, etc. Since lists are usually paid for each time they are used, it is beneficial to test the effectiveness of the list. This can be accomplished by making special offers that are given only through the mailing, and tracking how many new customers were created through these offers.

Businesses also create their own lists of existing customers. These can be used to help reinforce the loyalty of existing customers and increase the frequency of their purchases. Common items sent to existing customers can include:

- Greeting cards at holidays
- Customer "gifts" (usually trinkets with company information printed on the item, such as magnets, calendars, etc.)
- Copies of articles that may interest the customer (usually related to the type of products or services offered by the entrepreneur)
- Thank you notes or e-mails for large orders or referrals
- Newsletters (hardcopy or electronic)
- Special promotions only for existing customers
- Special announcements (new hire, new product, etc.)

Information to build a direct mail/e-mail database can be gathered from a variety of sources. Many entrepreneurs find it most effective to begin building the database at the start-up of the business. Information can be added on new contacts as the business grows. Data is also gathered to keep names and contact information as current as possible. Such database maintenance is best achieved by having a system that allows for easy and continuous updating of the database as new names and new information for existing names are collected. Sources of information for the direct mail/e-mail database include:

- Creating a basic form that is used to collect contact information on everyone who comes in contact with the business
- Fishbowl contests, where business cards are put in bowl to win prizes or free products/services, at tradeshows, events, or at point of customer contact
- Suggestion boxes
- Special offers, such as free newsletters or contests, that require people to fill out a form

ADVERTISING

Bootstrap marketing does not imply that more traditional methods of advertising are not strategies employed by growing ventures. Bill Evans, President of Evans Glass, was very concerned about the cost of advertising his glass business when he first considered expanding his advertising budget.[6] He had always tried to keep a bootstrapping approach to the business he had taken over from his father. Historically, Evans Glass used only word of mouth and yellow pages advertising, which cost about $3,500 per year. The business had seen level sales for several years. In 2001 he made the decision to expand his promotional efforts and include television advertising.

Bootstrapping plays a role in traditional advertising. First, as illustrated in the previous example, advertising can improve cash flow. After a careful test of its effectiveness, Evans Glass used a $100,000 investment in advertising to create a $1.5 million increase in sales and improve profits by over $200,000. Bill Evans always continued to test different ads and different placements to assure that this spending was effective.

After a very successful test of a few select television ads, Bill made the commitment to increase his promotional budget to $7,500 per month and launch a consistent ad campaign using local television stations. His decision to increase their rather modest advertising budget and expand his marketing tactics resulted in Evans Glass doubling in sales over next four years. Evans Glass's net profits also increased significantly from about 1 percent of sales to over 10 percent over this same time period.

To keep the costs associated with advertising agencies down, the entrepreneur can play an active role in the development and placement of ads. Also, start-up advertising agencies are eager to work for more reasonable rates than more established agencies. Some businesses find that using college interns who are advertising majors can also keep costs down, while keeping quality at an acceptable level.

TELEVISION ADVERTISING

"I started going to T.V. to brand and create awareness of our company because most people did not know what our glass company offered. It was to grow awareness," said Bill Evans of Evans Glass. "We sold a product that is hard to describe. It is a visible project. It is hard to describe a mirror or glass, so we decided not to do radio."

Although television advertising may not seem at first like a bootstrapping approach to promotion, the example of Evans Glass demonstrates that it can be if approached using a bootstrapping philosophy. National television ads can be extremely expensive. Depending on the viewers reached on a show, ads can cost hundreds of thousands or even over a million dollars for a single thirty-second spot. For most entrepreneurs, national advertising makes little sense, since most of the people it reaches are not likely to be potential customers.

However, local stations and cable channel ads can be targeted to reach a specific market at costs that can be comparable to other local advertising media. The proliferation of cable channels allows for a highly targeted approach that can be used to reach a very specific group of people. And cable channel ads can also be targeted to specific geographic markets. For example, Bill Evans runs most of his ads through the local feeds of the TV guide and travel channels. He found that these stations were most effective at reaching his target market of affluent, middle age homeowners.

Television also offers remnant ad times, which offer a low cost alternative that can be used to test the effectiveness of this medium for a particular business. Remnant ads are blocks of times that do not get sold in advance. Television channels are willing to sell these times at a steep discount. The purchaser of remnant ads cannot choose a specific time or show for their advertisement to run. The ad is placed at the last minute when unsold spots arise during the daily schedule. It is a low cost way to determine if a particular channel is effective in reaching the desired target market. If it is, the choice can be made to either keep buying remnant spots, or pay more to target specific times and shows that might potentially increase the effectiveness of ads.

NEWSPAPER, MAGAZINE, AND "EZINE" ADS

Advertising in newspapers, especially in larger cities, can be quite costly. Placement within the newspaper is important. For example, since men tend to be the main decision makers for the purchase of automobile tires, ads for tire stores are much more effective when placed in the sports section which men tend to read rather than in the food section which tends to get more female readers. Coupons can lead customers to try the business, while at the same time give the entrepreneur some idea of the ad's benefit in bringing in new business. With the explosion of news sources on the Internet, adults in their twenties and thirties tend to go to news sites on the Web for much of their news. The most common readers of newspapers tend to be older. Therefore the age of the target market should be kept in mind when deciding whether to use newspaper ads. Newspaper readers tend to be much more localized.

Magazine advertising is often even more expensive than advertising in newspapers, so care should be taken to insure that it actually can create new business. The advantage of magazine advertising is that magazines tend to be geared toward very specific interest groups. For example, a chain of private residential high schools relied primarily on parenting magazines for their advertising. While a single color ad cost them $25,000, they found that each ad created several inquiries from parents interested in their program. They also found that the more consistently they ran the ads in these magazines, the more effective they were in generating potential new customers. The consistency of their advertising built brand awareness among parents who read the magazines.

More publications are opting to bypass the printed format and are creating a new breed of periodical known as "ezines." An ezine is a periodical that is exclusively delivered via the Internet. The advent Web-based "ezine" publications have lead to a greater proliferation of publications geared to even narrower and more specialized target markets. These more specialized publications can create even more effective target marketing for advertising.

RADIO

Advertising on the radio can be highly targeted. Stations cater to fairly narrow demographic categories. Radio stations tend to attract a fairly specific demographic group. By knowing the age and socioeconomic status of the customer, a business can generally choose a radio station that tends to attract that specific target market. It is best to use only one or two stations whose listeners match the demographic category of the business running the ads, as there is a significant diminishing return to advertising on more than one or two radio stations. Stations will barter or negotiate pricing, especially to attract new business. Also, as radio listenership has plateaued, stations have had to become more competitive in their ad pricing rates to remain competitive. And like television stations, radio stations will offer remnant airtime at a steep discount. Remnant ads can be a good way to test the effectiveness of radio advertising on specific stations before deciding to a longer-term commitment.

SELLING

Every successful entrepreneur must learn to sell. In the start-up, it is often the entrepreneur who is out selling their business, first to prospective investors and employees when preparing to get ready to launch, and then to prospective customers once the business commences operations. Although the entrepreneur may spend less time selling as the business grows, the importance of selling only becomes more important to support the growing venture by adding on new customers and retaining existing ones.

BOOTSTRAPPING A SALES FORCE

If personal selling is part of the expectations in an industry, at some point the venture will need to employ full-time sales staff. Early on in the life of the venture the entrepreneur may be the only person selling for the business. But eventually, the demands of growth will require that the entrepreneur spends less of his or her time selling and more on growing and running the business.

The cost of hiring a sales force can be bootstrapped in several important ways. First, if the sales staff are employed, putting them on commission pay can help keep costs down until they become productive and start generating sales for the business. Commission pay is a common form of payment for sales personnel. It helps bootstrap the cost of building a sales force by timing the cash flow of paying these employees to the revenues needed to cover their compensation. A small base pay may need to be paid for sales personnel depending on competitive practices in the industry.

A second means of bootstrapping a sales force is to hire independent sales personnel, known as sales reps or manufacturer's reps. A sales rep is an independent contractor who sells for several different companies at one time (see Chapter 4 for more on independent contractors). Often the companies they represent are small to medium-sized businesses that cannot afford their own sales force. These companies all share the same target market. Sales reps may or may not sell competing products, but generally offer a wide array of complementary products produced by a variety of companies.

Some of the benefits of utilizing sales reps include the following:[7]

- Sales reps are not paid until they actually sell the product, which lowers the financial risk.
- Using multiple sales reps allows a business to enter several markets at once.
- Sales reps generally already have contacts in markets and good relationships with potential customers.
- Sales reps have experience in the market and can provide important market data on competitors and customers.
- Because they sell a wide array of products, these complementary goods can actually improve sales of a product. They often can be packaged together to make them more attractive than if each were sold separately.

As more businesses look to global markets, many are using sales reps to help build customers in foreign markets. Local sales reps have contacts with the local marketplace, giving easier access to local customers by having people represent the business who have credibility with local customers and knowledge about local market conditions. They know the local culture and can help navigate the idiosyncrasies unique to many foreign markets. Sales reps also can help expedite entry into international markets through their experience with local regulatory requirements.

Finally, even a growing venture can turn its customers into its sales force. Many customers will proudly wear hats, tee shirts, buttons, and do forth that show their allegiance to a business. And the benefits of word of mouth do not diminish as a venture grows. The same techniques to build word of mouth discussed in Chapter 6 also apply to growing entrepreneurial ventures.

SELLING AT TRADE SHOWS AND CONFERENCES

Trade shows and industry conferences can be an excellent place to promote a business and engage in personal selling to a captive audience. The key in attending such events is to find a way to get noticed while at the event and to assure that people remember the business after they return home from the event. Bootstrappers find creative means to attract potential customers while at an event. Since exhibitors at trade shows have to compete for the attention of the attendees, each element of selling through these events needs careful planning and attention to detail:

- *The display.*   The purpose of a display at a conference is to attract potential customers to facilitate making a sales pitch. Lighting, color, graphics, and pictures all add to the visual draw of a display.[8] Beyond catching people's attention with its design, the display must clearly and quickly communicate the key essence of the product being sold and its benefits. The message can be just as effective as the visual display in drawing people in. Contests, free give-aways, food and drinks, and other techniques can also help draw people in. If it's possible to have a working prototype of a product or a video loop of its use in the booth, this will help attract prospects. Some entrepreneurs will even go further to attract attention. Attractive models, animals, and entertainers have been used to rise above "the noise" of a trade show floor.

- *Staffing the event.* Although the display draws people in, the staff working the booth convert those prospects into customers. The sales pitch should be well-rehearsed and delivered with enthusiasm, sincerity, and passion. The time that a prospect spends at each display is very short. The people in the booth must focus on quickly:

  - Communicating the key elements of the sales pitch
  - Answering questions and addressing objections
  - Sorting out "lookers" from true prospects
  - Taking steps to assure future contact with all prospects

- *Follow-up.* Most contacts developed at trade shows and conferences will not follow-up on their own. Simply providing a business card or brochure is not enough, as the attendees will leave with a pocket full of business cards and a bag full of brochures. That is why it is essential to gather contact information on each prospect. Fishbowl contests where people drop in their business cards to win a prize at the end of the show can be an effective way to develop a list of post-event contacts. Sign-ups to receive catalogues or samples can also be effective. Some shows provide attendee lists to exhibitors. Experts recommend a quick follow-up after an event via e-mail, a phone call, or a personal hand-written note.

Even with their high cost, trade shows can actually be an efficient means of selling. For example, Dr. Jim Stefansic found medical conferences to be an excellent use of their limited marketing funds for their medical device start-up called Pathfinder Therapeutics. Such conferences allowed them to talk with a large number of physicians who would be key allies when selling their new product to hospitals. Such conferences also attracted venture capital investors. In addition to attracting future customers, Pathfinder was trying to raise about $5 million in venture capital. So although the conferences were expensive events to attend, the money was well spent due to the large numbers of important contacts they were able to make at each conference. But, they tried to use bootstrapping to help save costs associated with attending such events.

There are a number of ways that a bootstrapper can cut costs without diminishing the effectiveness of attending a trade show or convention. Travel costs can be the major expense associated with attending a conference to promote a product or service. Generally, such events are held in larger cities, often popular destinations that will attract more attendees. Although airfare to larger cities is often less expensive, the bootstrapper can still save additional costs by booking airfares through discount airlines or through Web sites that offer bargain fares through auctions such as Priceline. Hotel rates and meals are generally much higher in larger cities and at destination resorts. If the rates at the host hotel are not discounted enough, lower rates may be available through neighboring hotels within walking distance to the conference hotel. Again, many Web sites offer much lower rates through the auction process. Meals are generally the most expensive within conference hotels. Significant savings can be realized by eating meals in less expensive restaurants outside of the hotel. One entrepreneur interviewed for this book said he always made a stop at a local Sam's Club and stocked up food he could eat in his room to help save costs when attending conferences.

The costs associated with attending the conference can include registration costs, fees, and costs of being an exhibitor at the conference, and sponsorship fees. One of the first decisions involves how important it is to be an exhibitor at the event and have a display table to promote to conference attendees. Exhibitors pay a "table fee" that gives them a large table top in the exhibit area of the conference. These fees can range from a few hundred dollars to thousands of dollars depending on the demand for exhibit space and the number of attendees. Fees can also vary based on location within the exhibit space. Most exhibitors set up a display on their table or within the exhibit space they rent. Again, the cost for these displays ranges from hundreds to thousands of dollars depending on its size and special features such as lighting, video displays, etc., and the fees charged for hooking up to power and Internet feeds. When budgeting for attending the conference the cost of shipping the display to each conference also needs to be factored in.

At some conferences, the entrepreneur may decide that the fees for being an exhibitor and all of the additional costs may not be justified. Or it may be the first time at this conference, and the entrepreneur is uncertain if all of the added costs can be justified. In such a case it may be best to simply attend the conference and "work the room." Many good contacts can be made through the people one meets through attending various conference events. When we were growing our healthcare venture[9], we would always attend a conference the first time to assess whether the contacts we could make there were worth the cost of being an exhibitor at subsequent conferences hosted by that group. We found that only about half of the conferences justified all of the expenses associated with exhibiting at the conference.

If additional exposure is desired at a conference, the entrepreneur may choose to be a sponsor. A sponsor gets additional recognition to the membership for paying additional fees. It may be advantageous to sponsor a specific event, such as a coffee break or cocktail hour, to secure even more visibility and assure more contact time with attendees. Sponsorship fees generally also include exhibit space, and often the sponsors get the most visible and desired locations within the exhibit hall.

BOOTSTRAPPING DISTRIBUTION THROUGH THE INTERNET

Distribution of the product (also called the "place" part of the marketing mix) is how the product is distributed to the final customer. Traditionally, distribution has been done through intermediaries, such as wholesalers and retailers, which creates the chain of distribution from the manufacturer of a product to the final consumer. Each step along the chain of distribution adds to the cost of the product. For example, the manufacturer of a snowboard sells the snowboards in large quantities to wholesalers for $100 each. These wholesalers store the snowboards until a retailer places an order, selling and shipping the same snowboards to the retailer for $150 each. The retailer then sells each snowboard to the final customer for $250 each. Every step in the distribution chain adds costs to the product, including the cost to store the product, the cost of employees to handle the product, transportation costs, and general overhead costs.

A bootstrapping philosophy also applies to distribution. The Internet has created opportunities for businesses to both shorten and widen distribution channels with very little added cost. The Internet has also allowed businesses to create a *virtual niche* in the market. Traditional market niches have most often been defined at least in part by the geography of the customer community. However, the Internet has allowed business to create niches that are independent of geographic limitations. Through Internet based ordering, manufacturers can link directly to retailers or even bypass retailers going directly to the final customer. Through these strategies the distribution chain has been shortened, and the added cost created by intermediaries can be dramatically reduced. In the snowboard example, if the manufacturer sets up an e-commerce site that allows them to now sell directly to the retailer, the $50 added to the price by the wholesaler can either be added to the profits of those still in the chain of distribution—the manufacturer and retailer—or can be passed along as savings to the customer. Either way, the process has been made more efficient, which is at the heart of bootstrapping.

The Internet has also created the opportunity for businesses to widen their channels of distribution with very little added cost. Retailers are no longer bound by the definition of the market that is created by their physical location. They can engage in e-commerce to potential customers literally around the world through their Web site. For example, Eastern Boarder sells snowboards and equipment through its four retail locations in Massachusetts and one store in New Hampshire. However, they have been able to broaden their market without adding additional space to these stores or by adding new locations using aggressive online sales through their Web site.[10] They have used the Internet to bootstrap distribution to a much wider market with only limited additional resources required to build and maintain the Web site.

Conclusion and Summary

Market strategy has changed with the dynamic change in the American economy. The marketing plan has become the heart of business planning, as entrepreneurs must be able to attract customers within a dynamic economy. The marketing plan defines the relationship with the customer for a business. Bootstrapping plays an evermore important role in marketing growing entrepreneurial ventures as a result of the transformation we are witnessing in the American economy. Product positioning, promotion, and distribution are all a part of the marketing mix for a bootstrap marketing strategy in a growing firm. Part III of this book will shift focus to the key issues in managing a bootstrapped business from start-up through its growth.

Discussion Questions

1. Discuss how the changes taking place in the economy have changed the nature of marketing for growing ventures. How does bootstrapping relate to business and market planning?
2. Describe product positioning as it relates to bootstrapping. Develop a positioning strategy and positioning statement for your business. If you do not have a business, develop a positioning strategy and statement for your college or university.
3. Develop a plan to develop a direct marketing campaign for a new business, or if you already have one, use your own business.
4. What are the common forms of advertising a growing business? How can bootstrapping relate to each of these?
5. How has the Internet created a new distribution strategy for many businesses? Develop an Internet-based distribution strategy for your business or for a business you are interested in launching in the future.

Endnotes

1. Schramm, C. (2006). *The Entrepreneurial Imperative*. New York: Harper-Collins.
2. http://www.sba.gov/advo/press/07-12. html, retrieved on June 25, 2008.
3. Schindehutte, M., Morris, M., and Pitt, L. (2009). *Rethinking Marketing*. Upper Saddle River, NJ: Pearson Education, pp. 114–115.
4. Flamholtz, E., and Randle, Y. (2007). *Growing Pains*. San Francisco: Jossey-Bass.
5. Ries, A. and Trout, J. (2001). *Positioning: The Battle for Your Mind*. New York: McGraw-Hill.
6. Lambert, R., and Cornwall, J. (2007) "Evans Glass." United States Association for Small Business and Entrepreneurship, *Proceedings*.
7. Stansell, K. (2000, July). *Hire a Sales Rep to Peddle Your Wares*. Retrieved from http://www.inc.com/articles/2000/07/20157.html, May 5, 2008.
8. http://www.entrepreneur.com/marketing/marketingbasics/tradeshows/article172158. html, retrieved on June 24, 2008.
9. The author was co-founder and CEO of Atlantic Behavioral Health Care during the 1980s and 1990s.
10. http://www.easternboarder.com/store.browse.php.

CHAPTER

START-UP FINANCING AND DAY-TO-DAY CASH FLOW MANAGEMENT IN A BOOTSTRAPPED BUSINESS

I started the business with $5000 of my own money (from my previous job). That money was allocated towards a laptop, business incorporation, and initial business supplies. After that, my living expenses were covered by unemployment (since I got laid off by my previous employer) and my savings. After we exhausted those funds, we utilized loans from my wife's student loan availability. All of this helped me grow the business for two years without taking any income home. At the end of year two, I finally was able to bonus myself out a full year's pay. (Nicholas Holland, Founder of CentreSource)

Overview

Priming the Pump: Common Sources of Start-Up Funding

Using Bootstrapping to Be a Good Steward of Funding

A Note of Caution: Credit Cards

Managing Cash Flow in a Bootstrapped Venture

Conclusion and Summary

LEARNING OBJECTIVES

✓ Examine the interplay between bootstrapping and the common sources of start-up funding
✓ Reflect on the ethical dimensions of funding and the entrepreneur's responsibility of stewardship of the resources secured to launch and grow the business
✓ Understand the problems and limitations of a business owner's use of credit cards
✓ Examine techniques to help optimize the management of cash flow in an entrepreneurial venture

OVERVIEW

In the previous parts of this book, we examined the various tools, techniques, and strategies that entrepreneurs can use to bootstrap their businesses, ranging from decisions about overhead, to staffing, to operations, and finally to marketing. In Part III, our focus shifts to managing a bootstrapped business. Even a bootstrapped business needs some level of seed funding. This chapter examines the most common sources of financing in start-up ventures—including money from the entrepreneur, friends, and family. As has been stressed throughout this book, a fundamental part of bootstrapping is effective cash flow management. The second part of this chapter explores how entrepreneurs can overcome the challenges they face in managing the cash flow of a bootstrapped business.

PRIMING THE PUMP: COMMON SOURCES OF START-UP FUNDING

While bootstrapping can help reduce the need for start-up funding, almost every business needs some start-up capital. As stated in Chapter 1, a 2006 survey conducted by Wells Fargo Bank found that the average start-up financing for the new businesses they surveyed was $10,000.[1] This part examines some of the more common sources entrepreneurs use in order to secure the funding needed to get a new business off the ground.

FUNDING FROM THE ENTREPRENEUR

The Wells Fargo study cited above also found that 73 percent of start-ups were fully self-funded. That is, just like Nicholas Holland's story at the opening of this chapter, three out of every four entrepreneurs start their businesses with the money they have available from their personal sources of funding. For example, Nicholas Holland was able to build CentreSource, a high-growth Web development firm, using several self-financing techniques that are in one way or another quite common to many start-up ventures.

Like Nicholas Holland, many entrepreneurs draw upon their savings to fund at least part of their start-up. They may use this funding to buy equipment, inventory, or to pay other start-up expenses. Their personal savings may also become a reserve fund to buffer months when the business is not able to pay them a salary. My partners and I had to rely on our savings when we first started our healthcare company. Although it became a fairly large business, the first two years had tight cash flow. As the owners, we only received paychecks for about half of the months during the first two years of our venture. By having savings in place before we launched the business, we were able to maintain the lifestyle we had before we launched our own entrepreneurial venture.

Self-financing sometimes comes from utilizing credit that the entrepreneur is able to obtain personally. For example, if the entrepreneur owns a home and has enough equity built up, he or she can take out a second mortgage on a home. Or, if they own publicly traded stocks they can pledge them as collateral to back a loan. In the opening example, Nicholas Holland used student loans that his wife had access to as a source of money to cover personal living expenses. Because these are all personal loans, it is important to understand that even if the business fails, the entrepreneur will have these personal debts to repay. If they are unable to meet these personal obligations they run the risk of losing their home or their stock if they have pledged them as security. Some entrepreneurs who rely on personal debt find themselves facing personal bankruptcy if their business fails and they are unable to repay their personal loans.

There are three main advantages to relying on self-financing when launching a new venture. First, it is fairly easy to obtain funds this way. As with the Nicholas Holland story, many entrepreneurs actively save money in advance of the actual opening of their new business to provide a cushion for living expenses until the business can provide a reliable salary. For some businesses it can take months or even a couple of years before it can support all of the basic living expenses of the entrepreneur. This is a part of start-up planning that is too often overlooked by aspiring entrepreneurs. Creating a savings buffer and cutting back on monthly personal expenses (think of it as the entrepreneur's personal overhead expenses) can go a long way to assuring the survival of the business through the start-up period. Many experts recommend that a start-up entrepreneur has at least six months worth of basic living expenses covered by personal savings before launching a new venture.

A second advantage of self-funding is that it can help to avoid the need of bringing other partners or investors into the business. Once an entrepreneur adds partners, it creates a variety of complexities to the business. It is no longer just one person's business, meaning that a consensus is necessary around all major decisions. Partnerships in business can be one of the most difficult issues that entrepreneurs have to face, and yet very little is written about them. Most entrepreneurs only worry about them when they have already become a complete disaster. Who an entrepreneur chooses as a partner should be given as much consideration in business deals as the markets to enter. Partnerships that have gone bad are a major source of business failure, sometimes leading to the break-up of otherwise financially successful businesses.

Business partnerships can be very difficult and costly to disengage from once the business is operational. All potential business partners should think carefully about the prospects and the implications of working together. It is essential to have discussions with the potential partners about everything related and even unrelated to the business. Entrepreneurs should know a partner's hopes and dreams, endearing characteristics and annoying habits, ethics and values, and so forth. You will spend more time with these folks than anyone else in your life and it will be a relationship that the law will make even more complicated to terminate than a marriage. Entering into a business partnership on impulse or too casually is about as smart as entering into a marriage the same way. Every entrepreneurial venture that includes partners should work with an attorney to create a shareholder agreement *before* officially incorporating. Just as marriages can fall apart on the honeymoon, business partnerships can fall apart before the first sale is ever made. Figure 8-1 offers a set of questions that can guide discussions between potential business partners to identify potential problems and issues before the business is actually launched. Such a discussion often leads to a change of heart about entering into a business partnership.

Although most entrepreneurs do not think about it, a third advantage of self-financing is that it makes the possible failure of the business a somewhat less complex issue to face, as there are no business loans to repay or other shareholders (either partners or investors) to negotiate with in terms of any exit issues. Because many of today's entrepreneurs are serial entrepreneurs—they do multiple deals over their careers—a simple exit from a failure can allow the entrepreneur to move onto the next deal without any lingering financial obligations from the failed venture. Also, because no lenders or investors were part of the failed deal, the entrepreneur will have limited or even no real impact on his or her reputation. If the next deal requires outside funding, there will not be a track record of problems with previous loans or investments by equity partners.

The main disadvantage of self-financing is that it limits the size of a business that can be started and may limit the entrepreneur's ability to grow the business to its fullest potential. Most high-potential ventures require some external funding, usually through angel investment in the early stages and then venture capital as the business begins generating revenues. A typical venture of this nature will often require hundreds of thousands or even millions of dollars to launch and become operational. It is a rare entrepreneur who would have access to this level of funding from personal resources.

The experiences shared by Kevin Drake and Kevin Jennings in Box 8-1 illustrate a common method of self-financing a new venture. Both of these entrepreneurs have salaried jobs that they use for their living expenses. Both of them have new ventures that allow them to work during the day and grow their businesses in the evenings and weekends. Some new businesses need to be developed during the day hours. In this case, many entrepreneurs take on evening jobs, such as waiting tables, bartending, or working the evening in a business that runs with more than one shift. At some point the business will demand too much time to allow the entrepreneur to maintain two jobs. Hopefully this occurs at a time when

FIGURE 8-1   Shareholder/Partnership Assessment

1. Each partner/shareholder should complete the following assessment individually.

2. *The partners/shareholders should then sit down and openly, honestly, and completely share what they wrote down and why they responded the way that they did. Use active listening, that is, repeat what you think you hear your partner/shareholder is saying to make sure that there is a clear understanding.*

3. *Do not gloss over differences. In fact, those issues that that cause disagreement should be discussed until there is a resolution.*

4. *The common understanding that comes out of this process should be used to formulate your partnership/shareholder agreement with your attorney before you begin business.*

What is your vision for the business?

What are your aspirations for the business? Do you want to build an empire, create a lifestyle kind of business, reach a certain standard of living, etc.?

What are your *specific* goals for your business/career? Income/lifestyle? Wealth? Free-time? Recognition/fame? Impact on community? Other?

What do you want to be doing in one year? In five years? In ten years? At retirement?

What are your work habits and work ethic? Are they compatible enough with your partners/shareholders to keep the contribution feeling fair to all?

How much time off do you plan to take each day, each week, each year?

How much money will you put into the business?

How much do you expect to get out of it?

Who will be the president of the company? What roles will the other shareholders/partners play?

How will decisions be made?

What is your credit rating? Can you help to guarantee a loan, if necessary?

What if you get married and your new spouse gets a job offer in another city? Would you move away?

What will you consider to be real success in this business?

FIGURE 8-1 . Shareholder/Partnership Assessment (continued)

How would you describe your tolerance for uncertainty and risk?

How much financial risk are you willing to take with your new venture (personal assets, personal debt, etc.)?

How many hours are you willing and able to put into your new venture?

What are the nonfinancial risks for you in starting a new business?

How do you react to failure? Give examples.

How do you react in times of personal stress? How do you deal with stress in your life?

How much income do you need with your current lifestyle?

How long could you survive without a paycheck?

How much money do you have available to start your business?

Which of your personal assets would you be willing to borrow against, or sell, to start your business?

Whose support (nonfinancial) is important for you to have before starting your business (family, spouse, etc.)?

Core Values

List the core personal values that you intend to bring to your business (for example, treating people fairly, giving something back to the community, etc.).

Where do each of these core values come from (religious faith, family, etc.)?

Why are each of them important to you?

How would they be put into practice day-to-day in your business? For example, how will employees, customers, suppliers, etc. all be treated based on your values?

the new venture is able to pay the entrepreneur a salary. If not, the entrepreneur may have to rely on savings or take on some debt or equity funding as a bridge during the transition from holding a job while also running the business, to working full time on the entrepreneurial venture.

BOX 8-1 START-UPS ON A SHOESTRING

Don't Quit Your Day Job

Each of the five founders agreed to build Prium Investment Management by completely self funding the business and continuing to work our day jobs. Everyone knew that we would have to balance school, our day jobs, and the time necessary to operate the business. Time management and persistence have been extremely important to establish Prium. I normally try to catch up on my work over the weekend and often feel guilty if I take any down-time because there is always something to be done.

We have been very intentional about managing our costs. One main area we have saved a lot of money is by avoiding office space costs. We currently just have a UPS Store P.O. Box for our mailing address and use space at local coffee shops and bookstores to meet clients.

We do not have a secretary, so I have a second phone I carry at my day job. I normally have to let the voicemail take a message when it rings and return the call when I have a spare minute at work.

One friend setup our website for a fraction of the cost that he normally charges his clients. Also, another friend designed our logo and all of our print marketing materials. These two guys have been instrumental in helping Prium cut costs.

The majority of Prium's costs have been software related. Software is the main area where we have not spared expenses because we recognize its importance to our service and brand image.

The technology advancement over the past several years has made it possible for us to operate Prium as a truly virtual business. Our team heavily utilizes email, online documentation sharing, and virtual meetings to collaborate. In addition, Prium uses TD Ameritrade as the "custodian" of all client money and all client account actions are executed electronically online.

Prium's main marketing tool is word of mouth; we have not done a lot of formal marketing. We do use an email newsletter service that distributes all of our newsletters for five dollars plus one cent for every recipient. This email distribution tool allows us to track the readership and when the newsletter is forwarded to additional readers.

Each of the five Prium principles were originally paying a small monthly amount to cover operating expenses. However, Prium became self sufficient after 1.5 years and we no longer continue these payments. Prium has advanced a long way in three short years thanks to a selfless team, smart bootstrapping techniques, and a lot of hard work!

(Kevin Drake, Co-founder of Prium)

When balancing my business and my other job, I have to find out what kind of jobs will let me pick my hours. If I work on my business more at night, I need to find a day job. I try to find out when my clients need me to be available and then plan my other job around those hours.

When you get an internship, the company might think you are there to stay and get a job with them in the future. You have to be honest with what you are looking for. I tell them as far as working, to be honest, I am just there to learn.

One of the challenges is the time. I am doing so much. I am doing everything. With school and another job, the responsibilities of running a business are crazy. I find myself writing out policies about future employees, but I have to learn to concentrate on what is needed now instead of spending so much time in the future and on the bigger picture.

The biggest thing is prioritizing. Right now I am working at a call center. Even though that can be boring, I am sitting down at desk with a telephone. So, in between phone calls, I am working on our marketing plan and sending e-mails. Who I e-mail first is an important decision.

(Kevin Jennings, Co-founder of soundAFX)

Funding from Family and Friends

There are two categories of sources of start-up capital that typically fund start-up ventures: (1) investors who the entrepreneur knows personally, and (2) professional investors. No matter which category the funder falls under, those who provide an equity investment join the founding entrepreneurs as co-owners of the business. Unlike debt financing, which ends when the loan is repaid, equity investors are permanently (or at least semipermanently) a part of the business.

The most common type of investors for a start-up includes the entrepreneur's friends and family. Most estimates are that 85–90 percent of capital for small businesses comes from self-financing from the entrepreneur or funding from friends and family. Even in high-growth ventures, funding from these sources is typically about 80 percent of all start-up capital.[2] Family members provide funding for many different reasons. Some are motivated by altruism—they just want to help the entrepreneur get started and be successful. They may see it is a good investment with the potential for significant returns. Still others can be driven by greed—they see the investment as a way to ride on the entrepreneur's coattails to fortune and fame. But regardless of the reason they provide financial assistance, defined boundaries and expectations must be clearly established. Family business experts describe the importance of keeping boundaries clearly defined between business and personal relationships—business as business, family as family, and friendship as friendship. No matter what the motivation, funding from family and friends is often modest, requiring careful attention to bootstrapping to make the most of the limited start-up finding normally available from such sources.

When accepting funding for a business from family members it is critical that everyone involved fully understands all of the possible implications of the business relationship. Most experts recommend that the entrepreneur should never take money from a family member as a "gift." Instead, it should be set up as what is called an *arm's length transaction*—structured the same way as it would be with a complete stranger. The transaction should be treated either as a formal loan or as a formal investment.[3] The entrepreneur should present the interested family member a formal business plan, which should be discussed in full detail. The entrepreneur should review the business plan with potential family and/or friends interested in providing funding and make certain that they fully understand the risks involved with the business.

Any loan from a family member should have a formal loan agreement that defines interest rate and payment terms. An advantage of funding from family and friends is that the terms of any agreement can be more flexible.[4] For example, to help the entrepreneur, payments can be delayed if cash flow becomes tight. However, interest should always continue to accrue during this time and eventually must be repaid. The IRS publishes the current standard interest rates at its Web site, http://www.irs.gov/ (enter "interest rate" into its search feature). The published IRS interest rate is the minimum interest rate to use in any business loan. To avoid potential negative tax consequences including possible penalties in the future, no loan from friends or family should ever be structured without interest.

If the funding is structured as an investment rather than as a loan, the family member or friend is now the entrepreneur's partner. This means the partner has certain rights that any shareholder has in a privately held business. The partner votes on board of director membership and must approve certain major decisions about the business, such as a sale of the business. All shareholders must be provided with complete financial data at least once a year. The entrepreneur should strongly recommend that friends or family investing in the business consult with independent professionals (and attorney and a CPA) to fully understand any possible tax and liability issues that may arise due to the investment.

Most private businesses today are set up as pass-through entities, most commonly as Limited Liability Corporations (LLC) or sub-chapter S corporations (S-Corps). Profits are not taxed for the corporation, but instead the profits are assigned based on ownership to the shareholders. They then pay personal income tax on their share of any business profits earned each year. All of this should be made clear to all parties before any investment funds are accepted for the business. This includes a clear plan on how cash will be distributed from the business to share in the profits and to cover any individual tax liability that shareholders incur due to their ownership. Even if the entrepreneur plans to keep profits in the business to fund growth, it is advisable to distribute enough cash to the shareholders to at least cover any income taxes they will incur due to their ownership in the business.

Whether the money is treated as a loan or an investment, entrepreneurs should regularly communicate good *and* bad news. Entrepreneurs should provide regular quarterly or even monthly summaries that include any significant accomplishments, challenges, and major events. All of these steps will help keep issues that are business as business, and issues that are family as family. After all, Thanksgiving comes every year—it is best to avoid the potential of a business deal spoiling the family dinner.

PROFESSIONAL INVESTORS

There are two general types of professional investors who fund new entrepreneurial ventures. These investors generally provide much larger sums of funding and seek very high rates of returns. Their funding is made in what is called a high-growth, high-potential venture. It is important to note that even when considering only high-growth ventures, the percentage of funding from professional investors is still relatively small. A 2003 survey of the INC 500 (America's fastest growing privately held businesses) found that these high-growth ventures received only 2 percent of their funding from formal professional investors.[5]

The first type of professional investor is angel investors. Angel investors are wealthy individuals who personally invest a small portion of their portfolio in start-up and early stage ventures. Often, these individuals are former entrepreneurs who have exited their ventures with a large sum of money. Angel investors either make investments as individuals or band together in a network with other angels to pool their funds, making investments as a group. Angel investors typically invest $10,000 to $500,000 in any given business deal. The second type of professional investment is venture capitalists. Venture capitalists pool large sums of money into a venture capital fund from wealthy individuals and institutional investors (for example, insurance companies and retirement funds). Venture capitalists typically fund ventures that are beyond the start-up point, and are seeking money to fund a rapid and large-scale expansion. The typical venture capital investment is often in millions of dollars.

Both types of professional investors want to see a clear exit plan that allows them to recoup their investment and realize a substantial return, usually several times their initial investment. The timeframe for the exit is typically three to seven years after their investment. Since the passage of Sarbanes-Oxley, most exit events occur through an acquisition by a larger, often publicly traded company. Professional investors will want significant control over any business they invest in, often having the right to remove the entrepreneur as CEO if the business is not meeting agreed-upon performance goals.

As stated throughout this book, even high-growth businesses see benefits from bootstrapping. Investment from angels and venture capitalists comes at different points in time, known as *rounds of financing*. There is no guarantee if and when the next round of money will be secured, so bootstrapping becomes a means of managing what can become very tight cash flow between these investment rounds. For example, the initial investment (known as the seed round) typically helps the business get organized and is designed to carry the business up to the point that it starts to actually generate revenues. At that point the business seeks what is known as a *Series A* round of financing, which funds the business until it is cash flow positive from operations. The transition from seed-round financing and Series A-round financing is not always predictable and smooth. Therefore the entrepreneur may have to manage the business using a variety of the bootstrapping techniques discussed in Part II of this book to keep the business moving forward until the Series A money is actually secured and the money physically invested into the venture. Cash flow can become very tight during the transitions between rounds of funding, so bootstrapping is essential. Another benefit of bootstrapping for a high-growth venture relates to meeting investor expectations. Bootstrapping improves profitability by keeping overhead and operational costs down. For a high-growth venture with pressures for significant profitability from professional investors, bootstrapping can help in meeting these profit goals by optimizing the cash flow of the venture.

USING BOOTSTRAPPING TO BE A GOOD STEWARD OF FUNDING

In Chapter 1, we examined the general ethical aspects of bootstrapping. There is a significant and specific ethical dimension associated with the funding of a business. Entrepreneurs become stewards of the money invested into the venture. If the money is from self-financing, it is the entrepreneur's own financial well-being that is at stake. The money that is used to launch the business is at risk. This may include savings, investments, equity built up in a home, or retirement accounts. Also, the entrepreneur often is only able to take meager salary (or sometimes none at all) during the early stages of the business. Taking little or no pay from the business is known as *sweat equity*.

If the entrepreneur has a family, the magnitude of the responsibility becomes even greater. Joe Keeley, founder of College Nannies and Tutors, described it this way:

> While I very much try to keep what I take out of the business as minimal as possible, I have become frustrated by an entry level salary that has not kept up with my costs of living. I now have a daughter, so my family responsibilities are in tension with my business responsibilities. I still want to keep pouring any extra money back into the business, rather than increasing my salary . . . But I also have to think of my family.[6]

When outside funding is brought into the business, either from people known to the entrepreneur or professional investors, the level of responsibility and the need to be a careful steward of the monies put into the business expands even further. One entrepreneur described his experience when receiving funding from an angel investor:

> When it came time to close on the investment from our angel investor, I was taken aback when he took out his personal checkbook. There on the check was his name and his wife's name with their home address. I remember it was one of those standard checks with a farm scene on it— there was a little bluebird sitting on a fence post. I thought to myself, "This is the same checkbook that he and his wife used to pay his monthly personal bills." At the moment I looked at the check, I was struck by the fact that this person was about to make a very large investment in our business using his own personal funds. It immediately

brought home to me the responsibility we faced to take good care of this investor's money.

Bootstrapping helps the entrepreneur to become both more efficient and more effective with the resources available for the venture. This helps to make the entrepreneur a better steward of the funding entrusted to her by her family and her investors. Recognizing the responsibility associated with this trust to the people who have financially supported the venture helps assure that the entrepreneur is more likely to act ethically with these resources.[7]

A NOTE OF CAUTION: CREDIT CARDS

The use of credit cards as a means of bootstrapping to finance a business is almost legendary. A commercial construction company owner told me the story of how he used twenty different credit cards secured through unsolicited offers he had gotten in the mail to finance his business using cash advances on these credit cards. Within a few years his company grew to become a $5 million business. But not every story of a business started with credit cards has such a happy ending. From the *Wall Street Journal*:

> So after being turned down for small-business loans by banks because she lacked a business history and her business plan was considered too optimistic, the entrepreneur decided to use two credit cards—a Master-Card and a Visa—each with a credit limit of $8,000. And she maxed out both. "That was my leap of faith," says Ms. Babjak, now 42 years old.
>
> She had a bit of a hard landing, though. Ms. Babjak eventually had problems with the debt she took on and had to borrow money from family and friends to cover her payments. She learned from her experience, however, and now counsels other small business owners on how to handle credit-card debt more wisely than she did originally.[8]

Credit card use by entrepreneurs trying to bootstrap the launching of a venture is on the rise, and one study found that this is particularly true for women and minority entrepreneurs who may not have as easy access to traditional forms of start-up financing.[9] Credit cards can be easy to obtain. However, it may be too easy to attain these cards. The ease of securing debt with credit cards leads many entrepreneurs to bypass the important steps of opportunity assessment and business planning. Without careful market assessment and planning, the entrepreneur greatly increases the probability of failure. And if the business fails, the entrepreneur is still left with the financial obligations from any credit cards that may have been used to fund the business.

Credit cards have become almost indispensable in our economy. And for some transactions, such as travel expenses and Internet purchases, credit cards have almost become a necessity. According to the Federal Reserve, as of April 2008 Americans had $957 billion dollars in revolving credit (credit card debt is a major part of this figure).[10] One in three transactions and 40 percent of total spending in the United States is made with a payment card (credit and debit).[11] Credit cards are an expensive form of debt financing, with one-third of credit cards carrying interest rates of over 20 percent.[12]

Since the use of credit cards in today's economy is almost indispensable, it is important to make sure that credit card use does not turn into credit card abuse. Entrepreneur Eric Rosenfeld, founder and president of Adaptive Consulting Partners LLC, offers these tips when using credit cards in an entrepreneurial venture:[13]

- Don't use credit cards as an open-ended source of financing. Only borrow money that you know you can pay back with orders and work you already have booked. That is, manage it as if it is a line of credit that is only used to help with the timing of expenses with revenues.
- Take care in with introductory offers on credit cards. Shop around to find the best permanent interest rates and credit card annual fees.
- "Be frugal." Continue to bootstrap to keep your use of available credit to the minimum level.

MANAGING CASH FLOW IN A BOOTSTRAPPED VENTURE

The importance of bootstrapping to preserve one of the most precious resources of the business—cash—has been a recurring theme throughout this book. Cash is what allows an entrepreneur to stay in business, as it is the life blood of any company. It is important to repeat once again the fundamental philosophy of bootstrapping from Chapter 1: "Cash is King!"

Just because a business is profitable does not always mean it has adequate cash flow. There are three common causes that can lead to a profitable business not having enough cash flow to pay its bills on time. First, for some businesses, cash flow is different than revenues. Many businesses have to invoice their customers and wait for payment to arrive. Instead of getting cash at the time of the sale, the business issues an account receivable that may not be paid for weeks, or occasionally, even months. Some accounts receivable are never paid. Second, growing businesses that sell products will have to purchase inventory. The business will typically have to pay its supplier for this inventory within thirty days. However, inventory will take a certain amount of time to generate a sale. It may have to be processed if it is raw-material inventory. Or, it may have to sit on a shelf until a customer decides to purchase it. This creates a gap between the time when the business has to pay for the inventory from the supplier and when the customer actually pays to purchase that same piece of inventory. Third, the entrepreneur may have to pay for labor, supplies, and equipment in advance of the time that the goods or services are paid for. For example, a house painter has to purchase the paint and pay his workers to paint a house. And if he is new to the business, he may have to purchase brushes and ladders to complete the work. When completed, he delivers an invoice to the customer to receive payment for his work. Although he may have made profit on the job, he has had to buy paint and equipment, and pay his workers, all in advance of receiving payment from the customer.

In addition to the bootstrapping tools and techniques discussed in Part II of this book, there are some basic financial management tools that can help manage cash flow.

BARTERING

A transaction that trades goods or services for goods and services without the use of cash is known as *bartering*. Box 8-2 offers an example of how one highly successful business was able to barter the services from its business for products and services from another during the initial start-up. Other businesses have found they can barter their services for the use of space, access to technology, or for the use of equipment owned by another business. Because bartering is a "cashless" transaction, it preserves cash while still securing the resources, equipment, and services it needs.

MONITORING CASH FLOW NEEDS

The monthly balance sheet and cash flow statements do tell the cash position of the business. But these are static reports, only looking at the cash position of a business at a single point in time. These reports do not provide the specific details needed to make specific decisions. Cash flow is dynamic and requires continuous monitoring, management, and planning. If a business is experiencing cash flow problems, waiting for the standard monthly financial statements to identify the problem may allow the situation to unnecessarily escalate. Because standard monthly financial statements do not provide enough information when needed, entrepreneurs should develop systems tailored to their business that can provide the information needed to make informed decisions about cash flow.

BOX 8-2   START-UPS ON A SHOESTRING

Bartering

A bootstrapping technique that a lot of companies over-look is bartering. If you have a business that can barter, use it wisely. I have in my office about $16,000 worth of furniture and artwork. We did websites for businesses in exchange for the artwork and furniture they sold in their businesses. When a furniture company comes and says "Your bill is $16,000" I know they actually have 8000 dollars invested in that furniture. It has been easier for us to barter websites and get retail value for products in return. I bartered furniture, services, movie tickets, access to a company-wide event, etc.

(Clint Smith, co-founder of EMMA)

Cash flow problems are generally either a function of revenue- or expense-related issues. A common problem associated with revenues is that revenues are not meeting forecasts or budgets. Let us look at a restaurant as an example. The restaurant owner has bought inventory and made work schedules for the employees based on certain expected sales that are part of her budget. The owner monitors daily sales and finds that revenues for a given week are not meeting expectations. Because she knows this shortfall in sales is occurring as it happens, she can take steps to protect her cash flow in light of lower revenues. She might postpone and reduce some standing delivery of inventory since she has not sold as much of what she already has in stock. She may also cut back staffing until sales pick back up and revenues justify the need for more employees on duty.

Another way in which revenues create cash flow problems is related to accounts receivable collections. Collections are one of the most important, and at times most challenging, aspects of any business that depends on accounts receivable for cash flow. Of course, this is a particularly critical issue for the entrepreneurial venture that has to establish a foothold in its chosen market. In fact, there are two common mistakes that startup businesses make regarding accounts receivable.

One mistake is to assume that customers will automatically pay their bills and pay them in a timely manner. Customers may delay paying accounts receivable to preserve their own cash position. Such delays may be intentional or they may be due to ineffective systems of their own. Regardless of the reason, effective collection of accounts receivable requires these steps:

- *Create* a system to document invoices sent to customers and payments made on these accounts. Standard accounting software systems such as Quick-Books have the capacity to monitor accounts receivable. Whatever the system, it only works with accurate, consistent and timely entering of invoices and payments.

- *Monitor* the system to know who is paying and how quickly they are paying. Each month each account should be reviewed to see the size of the outstanding receivables and how long they have been outstanding. The common form of measurement for time is called *average days in accounts receivable*. It is important to monitor this measure for all of the accounts receivable and for each individual account to see where any problems may exist.

- *Act* on the information from the accounts receivable reports. Use it to contact customers who are behind on their payments. Set up a standard rule of when an account holder gets contacted, how they are contacted, by whom, and what is said. Methods of contact can include phone calls, e-mails, letters, or notices in future invoices. At some point, an account may require outside intervention to collect. This is can be through a letter from an attorney or turning over the account to a collection agency. It is best to wait on these methods until payment on the account becomes clearly in doubt. Most experts suggest that accounts over ninety days old have a very low probability of being paid, although this may differ by industry and type of customer (for example, some large national retailers can be notoriously slow to pay their accounts). Some businesses choose to hire a factor, which is a business that buys accounts receivable for a discount and then collects on them. Factors are an expensive option, often discounting an account by 5–8 percent of the account balance.

The second common mistake is to be more fearful of losing a customer than of not receiving payment from that customer. Entrepreneurs can often be too passive in their collection efforts, as they are concerned that if they push too hard to collect an unpaid account, the customer may stop doing business with them. However, if they are constantly not paying on time or disputing or refusing to pay their bills, the entrepreneur may be better off not even having them as a customer.

Entrepreneur and author Barry Moltz offers the following advice on collecting accounts receivable:[14]

- You are not a bank . . . Many of us are timid about collecting our money from our clients. It is a difficult topic to talk about, but if your company did the work or delivered the product then there is nothing wrong with asking to be paid. Don't be uncomfortable. It is your money and if you are to pay your own bills, you need to collect it.

- People respect what you ask for. Customers actually respect those vendors who recognize the need for cash and press hard for collections. This is not a sign of weakness but simply the sign of an entrepreneur that runs their company well.

- Customers that do not pay their bills are not customers; they are collection problems . . . . You should not do business with these types of customers. Do not continue to ship products or perform services for anyone who has overdue payments. It is your best leverage for them to pay you. Once the A/R is paid, ask for a deposit for the next order or insist they pay by credit card.

Expense-related issues with cash flow are often due to one of the following:

- unexpected price fluctuations from suppliers
- unanticipated expenses that were not built into the budget
- poorly managed purchasing processes that result in excessive expenditures that are not authorized nor required for the business
- timing problems—expenses payments are due earlier than expected

Cash flow information needs to offer up-to-date reports on the cash position of the business. But it should also look forward and help the entrepreneur understand the timing of cash coming into the business and cash going out of the business over various timeframes—at a minimum one week out and one month out. This requires modeling expected revenues, anticipated accounts receivable payments, and forecasted expenses to offer a full picture of future cash flows. The most effective means of forecasting cash flow is to develop a spreadsheet that lists day-by-day the expected payments and receipts that a business can expect and anticipated payments that are due, including payroll and payroll tax deposits. This can be used to project a daily forecasted cash flow balance. Figure 8-2 illustrates a simple example of such a cash flow spreadsheet for a hypothetical business.[15]

EMOTIONAL SIDE OF CASH FLOW MANAGEMENT

Especially for entrepreneurs using bootstrapping methods to finance their ventures, managing cash flow is more than just the technical decision-making on when and how to pay the bills of a business. There is a significant emotional aspect to managing finances. There is the stress that comes from the unknown. Will my customers pay me on time? Will our revenues grow quickly enough to support our growth? Will I reach positive cash flow before I run out of my start-up capital? There are also significant ethical issues associated with cash flow decisions. What if I don't have enough money at the end of the month to make payroll? How do I deal with my suppliers who are unhappy with how slowly I am paying them? The emotional fear of running out of cash is real. Poorly managed cash flow is a major cause of failure for entrepreneurial ventures.[16]

The stress of managing an entrepreneurial venture can take its toll on physical health of the entrepreneur and damage and even destroy relationships, including marriages. Therefore it is essential to address the emotional dimension of managing the cash flow of a growing venture. Here are a few steps that can help with this:

- Good information helps make good decisions. Use the tools from this chapter to help improve the information available.
- Be proactive and plan ahead. Surprises about cash flow trouble only heighten your anxiety. Early awareness of future cash flow trouble will allow for more options and usually better outcomes.
- Be open with others. Talk to your suppliers—they will often work with you and give you more time if you let them know in advance of any difficulties. Talk to your employees and partners—they may have solutions that have

FIGURE 8-2   Sample Cash Flow Forecast Template

Date	Expense Description	Amount Due	Expected Cash Receipts	Cash Balance
				$3,500
July 6 (Friday)	Phone bill	$100	$500	$3,900
July 9	Health insurance	$1,000	$2,500	$5,400
	Rent	$1,000		$4,400
July 10			$4,000	$8,400
July 11	Office supplies	$200	$6,500	$14,700
July 12			$6,000	$20,700
July 13	Payroll	$17,000	$2,000	$5,700

not occurred to you. Talk to other entrepreneurs—they have also been through such times and can put things in perspective.

- Bootstrap! The bootstrapping tools and techniques presented throughout this book can help prevent cash flow problems before they occur and can help reduce problems once they arise.

Conclusion and Summary

Self-funding from entrepreneurs and investments and loans from their friends and family are the most common source of funding for entrepreneurial ventures of all sizes and growth potential. Even when a venture receives capital from professional investors, such as angel investors and venture capitalists, bootstrapping plays an important role in managing the finances of the business. With all funding for a business comes an obligation of stewardship with the resources secured for the venture. There are several cash management techniques available to an entrepreneur to optimize the cash flow and address issues of timing with the disbursement and receipts of cash into the business.

Discussion Questions

1. What are the most common sources of funding for an entrepreneurial venture?
2. Discuss the potential challenges of receiving funding from families and friends. What are specific steps that the entrepreneur can take to manage the relationship of family and friend investors?
3. Explain how even high-growth ventures need to use bootstrapping.
4. Stewardship of resources secured for a venture is an important ethical consideration. Explain how this applies to self-funding, money from family and friends, and funding from outside professional investors.
5. Discuss the challenges of using credit cards in an entrepreneurial venture.
6. Interview an entrepreneur about the funding used to start the venture. Why were these sources used? What challenges arose with the decisions to use these sources of funding?
7. What are the common sources of cash flow problems in an entrepreneurial venture? Discuss the various techniques that can be employed to address cash flow challenges.

Endnotes

1. https://www.wellsfargo.com/press/20060815_Money?year=2006.
2. http://www.publicforuminstitute.org/nde/news/2003/enews-03-10-13.htm, retrieved on June 6, 08.
3. Ennico, Cliff (May 6, 2002) "Accepting Money From Friends & Family: 4 Ways to Get Your Cash Without Wreaking Havoc on Your Personal Relationships," *Entrepreneur*, http://www.entrepreneur.com/money/financing/loansfromfriendsandfamily/article51542.html, retrieved on September 11, 07.

4. http://www.eventuring.org/eShip/appmanager/eVenturing/ShowDoc/eShipWebCache Repository/Documents/Financing_Small_Bus.pdf, retrieved on June 6, 08.
5. http://www.publicforuminstitute.org/nde/news/2003/enews-03-10-13.htm, retrieved on June 6, 08.
6. Cornwall, J. and Naughton, M. (2009). *Bringing Your Business to Life*. Ventura, CA: Regal Books.
7. Ibid.
8. http://online.wsj.com/public/article/SB118524162516875639.html?mod=blog, retrieved on June 7, 08.
9. http://www.sba.gov/advo/stats/ssbf_98.pdf, retrieved on June 7, 08.
10. http://www.federalreserve.gov/releases/g19/Current/, retrieved on June 7, 08.
11. http://www.usa.visa.com/merchants/new_acceptance/benefits/index.html, retrieved on June 7, 08.
12. http://www.marketwatch.com/news/story/cardholders-caught-credit-trap-report/story.aspx?guid=%7B3995C83B-77A5-4DBB-83F1-04B07771CD52%7D, retrieved on June 7, 08.
13. http://eventuring.kauffman.org/Resources/Resource.aspx?id=33556, retrieved on May 1, 08.
14. http://eventuring.kauffman.org/Resources/Resource.aspx?id=33302, retrieved on June 7, 08.
15. For another example of a cash flow monitoring system see this site from the Kauffman Foundation: http://eventuring.kauffman.org/Resources/Resource.aspx?id=35210
16. Gaskill, L., Van Auken, H., and Manning, R. (1993). A Factor Analytic Study of the Perceived Causes of Small Business Failure. *Journal of Small Business Management*, 31(4), 18–31.

CREATING AND SUSTAINING A BOOTSTRAP CULTURE

From their very beginnings in Mike's basement, Mike and Charles have consciously avoided anything that they considered to be extravagant spending. Even as TAG became more successful, they chose to operate out of a moderately priced office space and to keep travel costs down by flying the discount airline Southwest and staying in hotels such as Hampton Inns for Charles and Microtel for the more conservative Mike. They believe that this approach to management benefits them as shareholders, their clients by keeping costs down, and the community by freeing up more resources to support charitable giving.[1]

Overview

What Is a Bootstrap Culture?

Steps to Building a Bootstrap Culture

Sustaining a Bootstrap Culture — The Challenges of Growth

A Final Note on Sustaining Culture: Leadership

Conclusion and Summary

LEARNING OBJECTIVES

✓ Understand the characteristics of a bootstrap culture
✓ Examine how a bootstrap culture is created in an entrepreneurial venture
✓ Explain how a bootstrap culture can be sustained over the life of an entrepreneurial business

OVERVIEW

Most of the attention to bootstrapping is on its role in start-up ventures. However, bootstrapping can be an important part of businesses that have become more established, including many larger organizations. Maintaining bootstrapping practices in a business as it grows depends on specific steps to establish and then sustain a bootstrap culture. This chapter examines the characteristics of a bootstrap culture, how such a culture is created, and how the culture can be sustained over time. The growth of a venture creates challenges to sustaining a bootstrap culture. Active steps by leadership are required to assure that bootstrapping becomes part of the culture over the long term.

WHAT IS A BOOTSTRAP CULTURE?

Chapter 1 presented nine reasons that entrepreneurs use bootstrapping in their businesses. Several of these reasons relate primarily to the start-up period of a business. But, bootstrapping is not just for start-up ventures. Three of the reasons for bootstrapping are particularly relevant for ongoing ventures. First, bootstrapping over the long term can help a business avoid the need to secure external financing and keep 100 percent of the ownership in the entrepreneur's own hands. By being more efficient throughout the life of the business, cash flow is optimized and the entrepreneur can build cash reserves that can be used to fund future growth. Charles Hagood and his partner in TAG (from the profile at the beginning of this chapter) have been able to grow TAG and more recently launch a new venture, Health Performance Partners, with no outside equity and very little use of any debt. This has enabled them to keep ownership control of their business and reduce the risks and limitations associated with taking on debt financing (see Chapter 8). They credit careful and prudent management of their resources and a continued use of bootstrapping throughout their growth. Through this, they have been able to maintain complete ownership control of their business. Mia Wenjen, founder of Aquent which is a leading talent agency for creative and Web professionals, describes the benefit of bootstrapping to fund growth this way:

> . . . [S]ince day one we've reinvested every dollar of company profits back into the business, to fund growth. This required extraordinary discipline as we opened branch offices, because once a new office became profitable, it seemed justifiable to "splurge" on items we did without in the start-up phase. Yet, we continued to run those offices leanly in order to invest profits into new locations and new lines of business. Our business model for growth depended on taking profits from mature markets to fund growth in new markets.[2]

Second, bootstrapping increases the income that the business can generate for its owners over the long term. It also helps them to build more wealth from the venture. Cash flow is what allows the entrepreneur to take income out of the business, and successful use of bootstrapping helps to generate more net cash flow. This is just as true in a mature business as it is in a start-up. The value of a business is based primarily on its ability to generate cash flow into the future. The stronger the cash flow the higher the value of a private business. Bootstrapping, therefore, helps build wealth for the entrepreneur by increasing the value of the venture by increasing its new cash flow over time.

Third, there is an ethical reason to continue bootstrapping over time. As seen from the opening profile of TAG, the partners in the business bootstrap to bene-fit their customers and their community by creating a business that can offer a fair price that generates enough profit to allow for giving back to the community through charity. This highlights the value of stewardship that was discussed in Chapter 8.

If a business is to sustain bootstrapping as it grows, it cannot rely only on the owners. Everyone in the organization must be a part of the process of bootstrap-ping the business. The most powerful means of assuring this occurs through building bootstrapping into the culture of the business. *The culture of an organi-zation* is comprised of beliefs and values common to those who work in that organization.[3] Culture also includes commonly shared assumptions about how people are expected to behave while working in the business. The commonly expected behaviors shared by all who work in a business are known as *norms*. Simply put, the culture of a business can be described as "how we do things in this organization."

Every organization develops its own culture over time. In an entrepreneurial organization, the culture begins day one from the values that the entrepreneur brings into the new venture. As the business grows, company culture is carried on through expected norms of behavior shared by its members. For example, if a part of the culture is that customer satisfaction comes above all else—even the profits from a particular job—employees know that they are expected to fix all problems and issues until the customer is satisfied with the job. Such behavior will not need to be explicitly directed by a manager, every employee understands that this is the way that their work is expected to be done. To put it simply, culture includes shared beliefs and values that are manifest in common behaviors within an organization. Culture is communicated by everyone in the organization and is sustained by employees over time through accepted norms, rules of behavior, and expectations.

In a bootstrap culture, therefore, the "way we do things around here" is to find creative and effective ways to achieve the goals of the business within the limited resources available. So what are the shared beliefs and values found in a *bootstrap* culture? To answer this question we must go back to the defini-tion of bootstrapping from Chapter 1—the process of finding creative ways exploit opportunities to launch and grow businesses with the limited resources available for most start-up ventures. Remember that bootstrapping is not just finding the cheapest way to do something. Rather, bootstrapping is about creating the desired impact using only those resources that are necessary to achieve the desired outcomes from marketing, administrative processes, staffing, and so forth.

The values and beliefs common to a bootstrap culture include:

- Frugality—it is desirable to achieve the same ends with the fewest resources possible.
- Creative solutions to the challenges of managing the growing venture.
- "Cash is King"—the cash in a business is its most precious resource.
- Stewardship—a sense of obligation to make the best possible use of the resources made available to the business from its stakeholders.

The behaviors that manifest these values and beliefs are the techniques, tools, and strategies presented throughout this book. Also, a bootstrap culture has several other benefits for a growing venture:

- It creates more opportunistic employees who have the confidence that they can use bootstrapping to find new ways to build value in the business.
- It pushes employees to maintain the creative edge, finding new and innovative ways to achieve the goals of the business within the limited resources available and to get access to resources that the business does not own or control.
- It reinforces an ongoing sense of urgency over complacency or inertia, which is even more compelling in today's dynamic economy.

In a bootstrap culture these behaviors become habits of all who work in the business. Members of the organization share a common understanding that bootstrapping behaviors are expected—they are the norms of how things get done around the company. These behaviors are modeled by the entrepreneur, and the entrepreneur creates expectations that bootstrapping should be followed by everyone who joins the business. As an entrepreneurial venture grows it faces forces that can lead to changes in its culture. The next section of this chapter examines how a bootstrap culture can be sustained over time even as a business expands.

STEPS TO BUILDING A BOOTSTRAP CULTURE

There are four steps that can be taken to build a bootstrap culture as a business grows.

1. ***Recruiting for a bootstrap culture.*** When bringing new employees into a business, it is critical to look beyond their technical skills and experience to fill the position. A fit with the bootstrap culture should also be examined. One approach is to develop open-ended questions that can be used during

the interview process. For example, "Tell me about a time when you had to accomplish a task when limited resources were available." If the interviewee answers the question by saying that she always had more than enough budgetary support in her old job, it might be difficult for her to adapt to a bootstrapping environment not having worked that way in the past. Or, if she answers by complaining about the availability of resources in her old job, or about how her old boss was always cheap, that is a good signal that the employee does not have bootstrapping as a part of her work ethic. On the other hand, if she speaks with enthusiasm and pride about how she got the job done within the limited resources available, she would more likely fit into the bootstrap culture.

2. ***Rewarding for bootstrapping actions.***   Rewards can shape behavior and attitudes of employees. Setting performance expectations centered on bootstrapping actions and decisions signal that bootstrapping is considered important. These expectations need to be built into the performance review process. Rate the employees on their ability to bootstrap and then reward those who do it well. In one company where bootstrapping resulted in better overall profitability in the business, the owner offered profit sharing to all employees making clear that it was due to their efforts to help control costs through bootstrapping. Rather than rewarding them for sticking to their budgets, the rewards were given to those who achieved the desired outcomes while spending less than had been expected by creatively using bootstrapping techniques.

3. ***Communicate a consistent message about bootstrapping.***   Highlight the importance of bootstrapping, in every type of communication ranging from informal conversations with employees to formal communications such as newsletters, annual reports, and policy manuals. A consistent message reinforces the importance of bootstrapping behaviors. For example, include a feature in every company newsletter about an employee who was the "bootstrapper of the month" and offer a story of how they accomplished a task with minimal resources. One entrepreneur described it as a process of "making heroes out of those who find creative and efficient ways to get things done when resources are at a premium." She believed that the strongest form of communication in her business was storytelling. She made sure to tell the story of bootstrappers in action and why they were so important to her business at every opportunity. Over time, these stories became such a powerful part of the culture that managers and employees told these same stories of bootstrapping to all new employees to help them understand the nature of "how things get done around here."

4. ***Actions speak loudly.***   The actions taken by leaders to bootstrap speak more loudly than what they say about the importance of bootstrapping. The company Fastenal has become legendary for its bootstrapping culture. Fastenal sells industrial and construction supplies wholesale and retail from its 2,160 store locations located in 50 states, Puerto Rico, Canada, Mexico, Singapore,

China, and the Netherlands.[4] Even with over $2 billion in revenues, the company's leadership takes bootstrapping actions that reinforce their culture. This story comes from a 1997 feature about Fastenal in *Inc* magazine:

> *[Robert] Kierlin [now Chairman of the Board] and chief financial officer Dan Florness could easily have taken a flight to a conference in Chicago, a little more than an hour away by plane. Instead, they drove five and a half hours in a van, saving Fastenal hundreds of dollars. They lunched at A&W, feasting on burgers and root beers. (Cost: $5 a person.) They spent the night at a motel in Rockford, a Chicago suburb, to avoid the high city prices. The pair even shared a room. "This sends a message that cost control is important to everybody in the organization," Kierlin says. "By being attentive to all expenditures, you can really set the example at the top."[5]*

When we look back to the example from earlier in this chapter about Charles Hagood and his partner in the company TAG, we see that they try to set the same example in their growing company by flying on discount airlines and staying in budget-oriented hotels when they travel. The example set by the leadership of a company is a powerful part of building culture. If the leadership is willing to bootstrap, it sends a message to the rest of the employees that they will be expected and encouraged to do the same. It can create a sense of equity within the venture. If the entrepreneur/owner is willing to do what it takes to bootstrap, there is a shared sense that it is not unreasonable to expect employees to do the same. Figure 9-1 summarizes the elements of creating and sustaining a bootstrap culture.

FIGURE 9-1   Creating and Sustaining a Bootstrap Culture

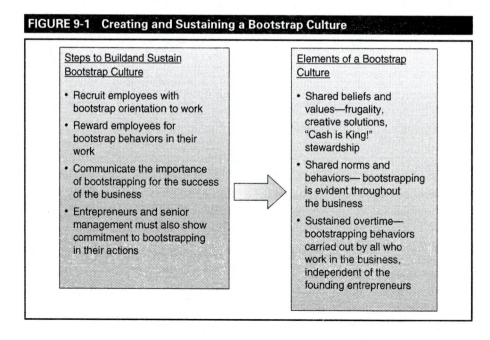

Steps to Build and Sustain Bootstrap Culture

- Recruit employees with bootstrap orientation to work
- Reward employees for bootstrap behaviors in their work
- Communicate the importance of bootstrapping for the success of the business
- Entrepreneurs and senior management must also show commitment to bootstrapping in their actions

Elements of a Bootstrap Culture

- Shared beliefs and values—frugality, creative solutions, "Cash is King!" stewardship
- Shared norms and behaviors— bootstrapping is evident throughout the business
- Sustained overtime— bootstrapping behaviors carried out by all who work in the business, independent of the founding entrepreneurs

SUSTAINING A BOOTSTRAP CULTURE–THE CHALLENGES OF GROWTH

. . . McCloskey discovered that bootstrapping got harder as he grew. When he started System Connection, he and his partners knew what needed to be done, so they did it. There was no money to spend, so they didn't spend any.... With 100 employees, things were more complicated. McCloskey couldn't simply pine for more "self-starters"; he had to direct people.[6]

As a business grows it faces several distinct challenges. Creating a culture that reflects the intended values and beliefs of the founding entrepreneurs can be of paramount importance in building a business that can not only survive the challenges of growth, but also thrive in its growth.

Sophisticated managers understand that their companies compete as much with their culture as with specific products and services. The CEO of a major New York Stock Exchange company once said that he could predict a division's organizational problems as soon as he had identified its culture. The ... challenge in building a successful organization, then, is to manage corporate culture so that it supports the achievement of the firm's long-term goals.[7]

If the entrepreneur intends to continue to manage the business using bootstrapping as it grows, then attention must be paid to sustaining the bootstrap culture created in the early days of the venture. In this section we will examine the transformation of the business founded by the entrepreneur as it grows from an entrepreneurial start-up into a sustainable business organization. There are four growth challenges that entrepreneurs face as they attempt to institutionalize and sustain a bootstrap culture:[8]

- The Growth Myth
- Resource Crises
- Culture Drift
- Leadership

THE GROWTH MYTH

American society takes pride in having the biggest buildings, the biggest homes, and the biggest businesses. Many entrepreneurs are influenced by this aspect of the American culture, assuming that they should grow their business as large as the market will allow. However, growth in revenues and market share often does not create more financial success for entrepreneurial ventures. Growth can be one of the most perilous times for an entrepreneurial venture. As any banker will attest, more businesses fail due to their inability to successfully manage the growth of their company than for probably any other reason. That is why bankers pay such careful attention to their clients who are experiencing rapid growth. They know the risks that growth can create. The strain on working capital created by increasing inventories and growing accounts receivable, resource needs such as new staff, and the need for more equipment and bigger space, all can create significant strains on cash flow. This can lead to a shift away from bootstrapping toward seeking large infusions of equity or debt financing.

The growth myth is that more revenues do not always lead to better profits and stronger cash flow. Bigger is not always better when viewed simply from the perspective of the level of revenues, market share, or number of employees. Growing a business with a cultural value of bootstrapping can help assure that the focus will remain on growing what really matters. It is profits and cash flow — and not revenues — that create value in an entrepreneurial venture and provide for its long-term financial strength.

RESOURCE CRISES

Managing a high-growth venture can become what seems like a constant pursuit of more resources — more employees, more space, equipment and furnishings, and the constant need for more cash to pay for it all. As has been discussed in previous chapters, many high-growth ventures can fail because they run out of cash. To meet the resource needs of growth, entrepreneurs often begin to rely more on outside funding and begin to pay less attention to bootstrapping the business and growing using internally generated funds. As one entrepreneur described it, "My growth created big cash flow problems that suddenly reached a crisis. I had to generate a quick infusion of cash to pay my creditors and meet my payroll if I wanted to make it to next month."

Ongoing business planning is a tool that can help to manage resources needs of a business as it grows. By effectively using financial forecasting in the plan, the entrepreneur is better able to understand and predict the impact of growth and the resources it will require. The business plan of a growing business needs to answer several important questions:

- When will new staff need to be hired? How much will they cost? How long will it realistically take before new hires can begin to contribute toward growth by either directly generating more revenues or creating systems and processes that can support growth?

- When will new equipment need to be purchased? How can it be paid for? Will it require more outside financing?

- What will the lag be between adding staff and adding inventory and the anticipated growth in revenues these steps will create?

- How will accounts receivable collections change as we add more customer accounts?

Business planning is not just an important activity for a start-up. For a growing venture the business plan becomes an important tool to understand the impact of decisions to grow. However, too many entrepreneurs expand based on instinct or even gut decisions rather than careful planning. That entrepreneur who described his cash flow crisis earlier realized too late how his crisis had occurred. "I rolled the dice. I decided that it was time to grow quickly and added on several new staff and bought new equipment without understanding how much it would all cost. I just had a feeling that it would all work." Unfortunately, it did not work the way he had hoped and he had to borrow a large sum of money at a high interest rate to survive.

CULTURAL DRIFT

Even if the entrepreneur has a vision for a business that is built on a bootstrap culture that culture can drift away from his intended vision as the business grows. Almost every new person hired into the business has worked in different businesses, often with very different cultures. That culture will have shaped how they have learned to behave in their work. The work habits that employees have developed in previous jobs do not end when they change employment—they bring those old work habits into a new job. For example, an entrepreneur in the healthcare industry was building a business based on a bootstrap culture. He wanted all of his employees to keep overhead low and unnecessary expenses to a minimum. He hired a marketing director who had worked for a large publicly traded healthcare firm, who brought with him work habits that he had developed over the several years at that big company. The bootstrapping entrepreneur wanted to keep administrative support to a minimum and so had always booked his own travel, scheduled his own appointments, wrote his own letters, and kept his own files and records. As the business grew, the marketing director started to build a staff that included clerical positions that booked travel, scheduled appointments, wrote letters, and kept files and records. This change in behavior in a leader of the business began to lead to a change in the culture away from the bootstrap culture originally instilled by the entrepreneur. As more and more new employees join a business, the culture can continue to be altered and drift away from the original vision of the entrepreneur. Each can bring in work habits and behaviors that can change the collective understanding of what is acceptable within the business—that is, change its culture.

Why didn't the entrepreneur stop the marketing director from behaving in ways that created changes in the culture? Entrepreneurs don't always understand that culture must be intentionally managed as the organization grows. And the demands of the day-to-day management of a growing business can lead an entrepreneur to take her attention away from the development of the culture in her business. It is not a conscious intent to stray from the original bootstrap culture, but more a case of benign neglect. Charles Hagood, founder of TAG, says that once a business moves beyond the start-up stage when bootstrapping is often done out of necessity, it becomes easy to get out of the bootstrapping habits. Once the cash starts coming in, everyone can tend to relax a bit. Everyone can get a little lazy, and start spending cash on things that are not going to create sales or take care of customers. Being prudent stewards of the cash in our business takes continued concentration and attention to details.

Together the flow of new employees with their old work habits from other jobs and the inattention of the entrepreneur to the venture's culture can lead to *culture drift*. It is rarely a sudden change in culture, but rather slowly changes with each small act, each specific decision, and each interaction with stakeholders, that cumulatively over time can lead to a significant and even fundamental change in culture. The bootstrapping mentality on which the business began can slowly, almost imperceptibly become lost over time. The healthcare entrepreneur from the example discussed earlier tells the story of how one day he and his partner were having a conversation about their business, when his partner said, "I hardly recognize this business any more. It is no longer the kind of place it was when we first started."

Leslie Brokaw compiled the following leadership steps that entrepreneurs often take to sustain a bootstrap culture even as the venture grows:[9]

- *"Adopt zero-based budgeting."*   The typical budgeting process builds each new budget off of the previous year. The budgeting process starts with what was spent during the prior year. The entrepreneur then decides on what percentage increase to allocate to each department or unit based on the goals for the upcoming year. When using zero-based budgeting, the entrepreneur challenges all managers to justify all expenses for their departments or units. No expenses are assumed to continue into the next year, including employee costs. The manager must justify each and every expense, including each salary line, and argue why each should be maintained or expanded into the new budget year. Zero-based budgeting is outcome-based, so the focus of budgeting shifts from securing the maximum amount of resources for a department to creating the strongest and most cost-effective department that can achieve the desired goals and objectives for the upcoming year.

- *"Consider each new project a start-up."*   When planning for a new location, a new product, or any other major initiative, the primary decision to move ahead should be based on a business plan. Just like a well-formulated business plan, there should be a market imperative for the new initiative. The initiative business plan should show what is needed for start-up capital and what returns can be expected in terms of added sales and profits, or expected cost reductions. Set up separate profit sharing and other incentive plans that allow managers to participate in the success of each new initiative. This increases their stake in the outcome, and challenges them to find ways to bootstrap to create better financial outcomes.

- *"Spread budget accountability throughout the company."*   Create autonomy within departments to take the necessary steps to meet the financial outcomes of the budget. Delegate responsibility to meet or exceed budget projections of profitability. Reward managers for reaching these goals. This will encourage them to find ways to bootstrap and optimize resources.

- *"Artificially restrict cash resources."*   Keep two separate cash accounts. One for short-term working capital needs and one for long-term cash reserves. Only put cash into the working capital account that is budgeted. In effect, out of sight is out of mind when it comes to the cash in the reserve account.

- *"Evangelize about bootstrapping."*   Brokaw offers this example: "Though Cabletron has grown to $290 million in annual revenues and has a work force of 2,300, it remains notorious for its metal desks, ratty cubicles, and bare-bones ethic. Benson, the president, and CEO Bob Levine claim to spend 20 percent of their time promoting and explaining the company's culture of frugality".

A FINAL NOTE ON SUSTAINING CULTURE: LEADERSHIP

If the culture of a business changes and no longer has bootstrapping values and its employees no longer routinely follow bootstrapping practices, it is possible to change the culture. The same four steps discussed in the previous section can be used to recreate a bootstrap culture. Recruiting, rewards, communication, and action by the entrepreneur all must be employed to rebuild a bootstrap culture. However, changing the culture of a business can be difficult and should be approached with a long-term commitment. That is why it is important to catch any drift away from a bootstrap culture as early as possible, before new values and behaviors get deeply rooted among employees.

The challenges that can result from the growth myth, resource crises, and culture drift can create crises in leadership in growing entrepreneurial ventures. The entrepreneur must provide the leadership for the business as it transitions through the technical aspects of its growth, such as planning for resource needs and taking steps to sustain the bootstrap culture.

As the business grows, one of the key roles of the entrepreneur as leader is to provide a relentless focus on the vision for the venture.[10] If growth through bootstrapping is a fundamental aspect of that vision, the entrepreneur must consistently communicate about the importance of bootstrapping the venture as it grows. Each key decision and major initiative should be explicitly made within a discussion and consideration of the impact of sustaining bootstrapping in the business. This helps to shape the behavior of managers so that they begin to make decisions within that same bootstrapping context as more responsibility gets delegated to them. As discussed above, the entrepreneur must also take clear steps to lead by example. The entrepreneur's bootstrap values should be translated into policies and practices, which then will more likely lead to bootstrapping actions. By modeling this behavior and institutionalizing it within the organization, the entrepreneur is able to lead the business with bootstrapping integrated throughout the venture. Figure 9-2 summarizes the leadership process that leads to a bootstrap culture and to bootstrapping in action.

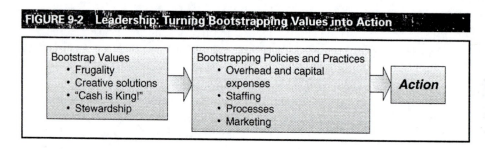

FIGURE 9-2 Leadership: Turning Bootstrapping Values into Action

Conclusion and Summary

This book has presented a dynamic model of bootstrapping that applies to small businesses and high potential ventures, start-up firms, and mature organizations. Maintaining bootstrapping practices over time is built on specific steps to establish and then sustain a bootstrap culture. Bootstrapping begins with the values of the entrepreneur. These bootstrap values become tangible through the establishment of policies and practices embraced by everyone who works in the business. And it is only through clear policies and practices that bootstrapping can be turned into action. Bootstrapping includes finding ways to achieve desired business goals and objectives when start-up capital is limited, minimizing the need for outside financing (debt and equity), maximizing the impact of funding invested by the entrepreneur, and methods for optimizing cash flow. All of these aspects of bootstrapping can help ensure the financial success of an entrepreneurial venture throughout all stages of its development and growth.

Discussion Questions

1. Why is it important to keep bootstrapping as a business grows?
2. Describe the three values and beliefs common in a bootstrap culture.
3. Explain the four challenges to sustaining a bootstrap culture in a growing venture.
4. What are the four key steps that can be taken to help build and sustain a bootstrap culture?
5. Explain the role of leadership in creating and sustaining a bootstrap culture.

Endnotes

1. Cornwall, J. (2006) "TAG." United States Association for Small Business and Entrepreneurship, *Proceedings*.
2. http://www.inc.com/articles/2001/06/22952.html, retrieved on June 9, 2008.
3. Deal, T. and Kennedy, A. (1982). *Corporate Cultures*. Reading, MA: Addison-Wesley.
4. http://www.fastenal.com/.
5. http://www.inc.com/magazine/19971001/1336_pagen_2.html, retrieved on June 11, 2008.
6. http://www.inc.com/magazine/19931101/3767.html, retrieved on June 10, 2008.

7. Flamholtz, E., and Randle, Y. (2007). *Growing Pains.* 4th edition. San Francisco: Jossey-Bass, p. 22.
8. Cornwall, J. and Naughton, M. *Bringing Your Business to Life.* Ventura, CA: Regal Books, 2008.
9. http://www.inc.com/magazine/19920901/4287_pagen_5.html, retrieved on June 13, 2008.
10. Flamholtz, E., and Randle, Y. (2007). *Growing Pains.* 4th edition. San Francisco: Jossey-Bass.

INDEX